SS-Freiwilligen-Grenadier-Division "30 Januar"

The 32nd SS Freiwilligen-Grenadier-Division "30.Januar"

Rolf Michaelis

Schiffer Military History
Atglen, PA

Book translation by Christine Wisowaty

Book Design by Ian Robertson.

Library of Congress Control Number: 2008933204

Printed in China.
ISBN: 978-0-7643-3101-5

This book was originally published in German under the title
Kampf und Untergang der 32.SS-Freiwilligen-Grenadier-Division "30.Januar"
by Michaelis-Verlag

Published by Schiffer Publishing Ltd.
4880 Lower Valley Road
Atglen, PA 19310
Phone: (610) 593-1777
FAX: (610) 593-2002
E-mail: Info@schifferbooks.com.
Visit our web site at: www.schifferbooks.com
Please write for a free catalog.
This book may be purchased from the publisher.
Please include $5.00 postage.
Try your bookstore first.

In Europe, Schiffer books are distributed by:
Bushwood Books
6 Marksbury Avenue
Kew Gardens
Surrey TW9 4JF, England
Phone: 44 (0) 20 8392-8585
FAX: 44 (0) 20 8392-9876
E-mail: Info@bushwoodbooks.co.uk.
Visit our website at: www.bushwoodbooks.co.uk
Free postage in the UK. Europe: air mail at cost.
Try your bookstore first.

Contents

Foreword

To this day there is no extensive publication on the *32. SS-Freiwilligen-Grenadier-Division "30. Januar,"* which was established in the spring of 1945 to reinforce the newly formed *Heeresgruppe* Weichsel. This is probably because this division, which was occupied with personnel, unlike any other new formation of the *Waffen-SS* in the previous months, lasted only approximately twelve weeks. Contemporary documents, such as, for example, a war journal, have not yet emerged.

The foundation of this publication is primarily the recollections from former members of the division, whereby special thanks goes to Eberhard Baumgart, Günter Adam, and Jochen Polle. The latter also provided photographs from Vogelsang. I would like to thank Mr. Steinemer from Belgium for providing the original documents.

Due to insufficient resources, this work cannot be entirely complete. Certainly, things could be added here or there. Unfortunately, with the resources available, a more in depth version was not possible. A special thanks goes to everyone who helped me publish this documentation.

Erlangen, April 1993
Rolf Michaelis

1

The Situation on the Oder in January/February 1945[1]

On 12 January 1945, at 0130 hours the Soviet spring offensive began. The Soviets had 32,000 artillery, 163 rifle divisions, and 6,460 tanks at their disposal. After a five-hour artillery barrage, rifle divisions supported by tanks attacked. After just several hours the German Front collapsed in multiple locations. On 13 January 1945, the 1st Belarusian Front under Marshal Zhukov attacked the German *9. Armee* at Warsaw with 31 rifle divisions and 5 independent tank corps from Soviet Vistula bridgeheads. On 14 January an attack was carried out with 54 rifle divisions, 6 tank corps, and 1 cavalry corp of the 2nd Belarusian Front under Marshal Rokossowskij against the *2. Armee* in Narew.

The soldiers of the *9. Armee* were able to stop the Russians' first wave of attacks until the Polish capital was surrounded by encirclement attacks on 15 January 1945. Without Hitler's consent, the *Oberbefehlshaber* of the *9. Armee*, *General der Panzertruppe* Freiherr von Lüttwitz, left the city and was subsequently discharged. His successor became *General der Infanterie* Theodor Busse.

By evading the German *XXXXVI. Panzerkorps* in the region north of Warsaw, the Russian troops were able to march directly toward the west. On 18 January Russian tanks reached Kutno, and on 20 January Hohensalza [today Inowrocław in Poland]. On 21 January 1945, Hitler ordered the army groups to be renamed. The *Heeresgruppe Mitte* became *Heeresgruppe Nord* (*Heeresgruppe Nord* had become *Heeresgruppe Kurland*), the *Heeresgruppe A* became *Heeresgruppe Mitte*, and the *Heeresgruppe Weichsel* (*Oberbefehlshaber*: *Reichsführer-SS* Himmler) developed from both of these.

Regardless of the remaining "Festungen" (strongholds), such as Bromberg [today Bydgoszcz in Poland] (captured by the Russians on 22 January), Thorn [today Toruń in Poland] and Posen [today Poznań in Poland] (on 23 February), and Graudenz [today Grudziądz in Poland] (on 6 March), the Soviets advanced toward the west through the "*Generalgouvernement*" and the "Reichsgau Wartheland." On 26 January the Soviets stood on its western border. This "Warthegau" was formed in 1939 after the Poland campaign. The Polish population was driven into the *Generalgouvernement* located to the east, and ethnic German settlers (primarily from Bessarabia, Bukovina, Hungary, and the Baltic States) moved into unoccupied farmsteads. The ethnic Germans in Wartheland who wanted to flee from the Soviets no longer knew where to go, because their previous homes had also already been occupied by the Soviets.

Soviet troops invaded Schneidemühl [today Piła in Poland] at the end of January 1945 and overran the so-called "Oder-Warthe-Stellung" [Oder-Warthe Line]. This location had been built up since autumn 1944 and offered excellent defense opportunities with its concrete bunkers, wire entanglements, and tank traps. It ran south from Landsberg [today Gorzów Wielkopolski in Poland] along the Obra for 75 km to the Oder between Krossen [today Krosno Odrzańskie in Poland] and Züllichau [today Sulechów in Poland]. Even during peace years the Obra line was provided with the strongest concrete bunkers, and had been reinforced more strongly than the Siegfried Line! Few *Volkssturmbataillone* from various sections of the Reich were available for war occupation as of 20 January. They were hardly armed and did not possess equipment and uniforms. The *Volkssturmbataillone* that were normally subordinate to *Gauleitungen* were used in such circumstances!

Because the *Oberkommando* of the army assumed that in an attack on Berlin a Soviet focal point would develop at Küstrin, this city was declared a stronghold. The severely war-disabled *Generalmajor* Raegener was appointed *Festungskommandant* on 25 January. Fairly fit for service, *Alarmeinheiten*, *Polizeieinheiten*, and *Volkssturmeinheiten* were placed in Küstrin. On 30 January advance parties of the *2. Garde-Panzer-Armee* and the *5. Stoßarmee* proceeded to Küstrin from the northeast. Two days later they had broken through the protective block in front of the city and reached the Oder.

In the eyes of the *Oberkommando* of the army the garrison town of Frankfurt/Oder was the second source of threat. Just like in Küstrin, there were no troops of fighting strength, thus *Kampfgruppen* were formed from military convalescents, those on leave from the Front, stragglers, and *Volkssturm*. Not until later did sections of the *434. Infanterie-Division* come into the city. Altogether, the "Festung Frankfurt/Oder" amounted to approximately 25,000 men, with roughly 100 Russian and French artillery. *Oberst* Biehler became *Festungskommandeur*.

In the first days of February 1945 the Soviets formed bridgeheads in Vogelsang, in Göritz, between Schaumburg and Kienitz, and in Schwetzig. For this reason, the idea to put a stop to the Soviets on the Oder was given up just as quickly as at the Oder-Warthe-Stellung shortly beforehand. However, Stalin then prevented a continued advance. He initially wanted to secure the right flank in Pomerania, and for this purpose full attack operations did not take place in the Küstrin-Frankfurt/Oder-Fürstenberg region. As of mid-March so many Soviet troops had assembled that from the German side it was no longer considered possible.

2

The *Divisionskommandeure* of the *32. SS-Freiwilligen-Grenadier-Division "30. Januar"*[24]

Johannes Mühlenkamp was born on 9 October 1910, in Metz (Lorraine). In September 1934 he joined the *SS-Standarte* "Germania." After graduating the *SS-Junker-Schule* Braunschweig and the promotion to *SS-Untersturmführer*, he took over the *Aufklärungs-Abteilung* "Das Reich." On 3 September 1943, he received the Knight's Cross to the Iron Cross as *SS-Sturmbannführer* and *Kommandeur des SS-Panzerregiments 5*. After the official position as *Divisionskommandeur der 5. SS-Panzerdivision* "Wiking," in which he was honored with the Oak Leaves to the Knight's Cross on 21 September 1944, he became *Inspekteur der Panzertruppen* of the *Waffen-SS* in the *SS-Führungshauptamt*. In personal union, from 26 January until 5 February 1945, he led the *Aufstellungsstab* of the *SS-Division "30. Januar."*

Joachim Richter was born on 28 July 1896, in Magdeburg. He participated in World War I as *Leutnant* in the *Fußartillerie*. In 1939 he joined the *SS-Verfügungstruppe* with the rank of *SS-Hauptsturmführer*. At the beginning of 1943 he took over the *SS-Panzer-Artillerie-Regiment 5*, in which he was honored with the Knight's Cross to the Iron Cross on 23 February 1944, as *SS-Obersturmbannführer*. From 5 February to 17 February 1945, he led the *SS-Panzergrenadier-Division "30. Januar"* as *SS-Standartenführer*.

Adolf Ax was born on 23 June 1906, in Mouscron (Flanders). In 1930 he joined the SS, and in 1935 became *SS-Obersturmführer* in the *SS-Standarte* "Germania." On 9 November 1942, he was promoted to *SS-Obersturmbannführer*, and on 9 November 1943, to *SS-Standartenführer*. As of 17 January 1945, he led the *15.* (Latvian) *SS-Division* as *SS-Oberführer*, for which he received the Knight's Cross to the Iron Cross retroactively on 8 May 1945. On 17 February he took over the *SS-Panzergrenadier-Division "30. Januar."*

Hans Kempin was born in 1913, and in 1934 belonged to the *Junker* of the first course of instruction at the *SS-Junkerschule* Tölz. He was *Kompaniechef* and *Bataillonskommandeur* in the regiments "Deutschland" and "Der Führer" until he became *Kommandeur* of the *SS-Panzer-Grenadier-Schule* Kienschlag in 1943. In mid-March he became *Divisionskommandeur der 32. SS-Freiwilligen-Grenadier-Division "30. Januar."*

3

The Formation of the *SS-Division "30 Januar"*

On 26 January 1945, shortly after Himmler's appointment to *Oberbefehlshaber* of the *Heeresgruppe* Weichsel, the *SS-Führungshauptamt* ordered the formation of the *SS-Panzergrenadier-Division "30. Januar"* at the Kurmark (Lieberose-Jamlitz) training area. The name "*30. Januar*" was chosen because the date of the formation fell during the period of the 12th anniversary of Hitler's seizure of power, 30 January 1933.

It became a troop of the last hour.

The *Ersatzheer* moved to the Front. With this, something happened that clearly displayed that the last reserves of the Greater German Reich were depleted: single units of the *Ersatzheer*—the various replacement and training battalions and regiments, as well as the schools that trained the replacements for the respective formations far away from the Front—became Front units.

From the interpretation of approximately 1,600 dates of birth of the members of the Division "30. Januar" ("Vermisstenbildlisten" (MIA books) of the German Red Cross, as well as original "Personalverfügungen" of the *Division "30. Januar"* and *Regiment* "Schill") the following age groups emerged:

Approximately 75% of the soldiers were 17 to 24 years old, of which 2/3 were 18-19 years old, approximately 15% were 35 to 45 years old, and the remaining 10% were marginal.

It was also clear that hardly any members were 25 to 35 years old, an age at which a soldier is physically and mentally robust.

The 34-year-old *SS-Standartenführer* Rudolf Mühlenkamp was assigned with the command of the *Aufstellungsstab*. After he performed as *Inspekteur der Panzertruppen* in the *SS-Führungshauptamt*, he led the *Aufstellungsstab* in a personal union.

On 25 February 1945, the division, which was initially intended as a *SS-Panzergrenadier-Division*, was changed to a *SS-Freiwilligen-Grenadier-Division* (horse-drawn) due to the extremely poor fuel situation. It consisted of:

SS-Freiwilligen-Grenadier-Regiment 86 "Schill"

In the summer of 1944 *Regiment* "Schill" was formed as a *Panzergrenadier-Regiment* (*Alarmeinheit*) from the *SS-Panzer-Grenadier-Schule Kienschlag* at the Bohemia SS military training area. It consisted of members of the *Panzer-Grenadier-Lehr-Regiment* of the school, the *SS-Pionier-Schule Hradischko*, the *SS-Panzerjäger-Schule Benešov*, and the *SS-Panzer-Grenadier-Ersatz-Bataillon 10* in Brno.

The *III. Bataillon* of the *SS-Panzer-Grenadier-Lehr-Regiment* was renamed *II. Bataillon*. Under the command of the previous *Kommandeur der Lehrgruppe* B of the Kienschlag school, *SS-Sturmbannführer* Klotz, after the assignment of a battery, the regiment was transferred to Slovakia for the suppression of the Slovakian national uprising.

At the beginning of February 1945 "Schill" was placed under the command of the *SS-Division "30. Januar,"* which was already in formation, as second grenadier regiment, and on 25 February reorganized into the *SS-Freiwilligen-Grenadier-Regiment* 86 and so named. This signified that the regiment was no longer motorized, but rather horse-drawn. It consisted of two battalions, 4 companies to each, and also the *13. Kompanie* and *14. Kompanie*.

SS-Freiwilligen-Grenadier-Regiment 87 "Kurmark"

As of 25 January 1945, *Regiment* "Kurmark" was formed within five days at the Kurmark military training area. First *Kommandeur* was *SS-Standartenführer* Anhalt, and after he was injured, *SS-Sturmbannführer* Vollmer. The regiment was initially named after its origin "Regiment Kurmark" and shortly later after the *Kommandeur* "Regiment Vollmer." It consisted of:

1) permanent staff and recruits from the Kurmark SS military training area (recruit depot), as well as from *Grenadier-Ersatztruppenteile* from the military training area (garrisons: Lieberose, Grünow, Guben-Neuzelle);

2) members of the *Kampfgruppe "SS-Waffen- und Unterführerschule Lauenburg/ Pomerania"*;

3) members of the *Waffen-SS* on leave from the front in Frankfurt/Oder, who wanted to go back to their units east of the Oder, particularly to East Prussia and Posen [today Poznań in Poland];

4) members of the *SS-Panzer-Grenadier-Ersatz-Bataillon* and *Ausbildungsbataillon 1* in Spreenhagen;

5) members of the *SS-Grenadier-Ersatz-Bataillon 9* in Stralsund;

6) and members of the *SS-Grenadier-Ersatz-Bataillon 16* in Senftenberg.

For a short period of time it was also named *SS-Regiment 32* (*1. Grenadier-Regiment* of the *SS-Division "30. Januar."*

As of 25 February the regiment was named *SS-Freiwilligen-Grenadier-Regiment 87* "Kurmark."

SS-Freiwilligen-Grenadier-Regiment 88[3]

In March 1945 this regiment was formed from *Kampfgruppe* Becker (the later *I./88*) and sections of the *I. Bataillon* of the *Polizei-Regiment 34* of the *Ordnungspolizei*, as well as members of the army and *Volkssturm* (as *II./88*).

Kampfgruppe Becker was formed in February 1945 with 900 men from the *SS-Führerschule des Wirtschafts- und Verwaltungdienstes* in Arolsen under the command of the tactics instructor, *SS-Sturmbannführer* Becker.

The Arolsen School was originally organized into a *Schulkommando*, two *Lehrgruppen*, and eight *Inspektionen*. *Lehrgruppe* A was a specialist group, while *Gruppe* B was purely military with an added *Zugführer* course. The teaching staff of the school consisted of approximately 70 *Führer*—the normal occupancy amounted to 1,100 men. Practically all weapons of the school were given to *Kampfgruppe* Becker. In March/April 1945 the unit was integrated into the division. This formation revealed how the leadership desperately attempted to form new units. In this case, accountants were put into action as grenadiers.

SS-Artillerie-Regiment 32

The *Artillerie-Regiment* was formed on 30 January 1945. The *Regimentsstab* came from the *SS-Artillerie-Schule I* in Glau, by Trebbin. The *I. Abteilung* and *III. Abteilung* were placed with the *SS-Artillerie-Ausbildungs-und Ersatz-Regiment* (SS-AAER) *Prag*. The *II. Abteilung* was formed at the Kurmark SS military training area. A heavy detachment with two *Gefechtsbatterien* from Sedlčany initially became *SS-Art. Abt. 550* and later the *IV./32*.

SS-Pionier-Bataillon 32[4]

From the *SS-Pionier-Schule Hradischko* by Prague the first members set out from Benešov on 28 January 1945. During the formation of the *SS-Pionier-Bataillon* 32 in RAD-Lager Fünfeichen they formed the staff and two companies. The third company was formed directly in Fünfeichen from Hungary and Romania, whereby only the *Kompanieführer* and an interpreter spoke German. During the first mission this company defected to the Soviets. They left behind only several discarded pieces of equipment. A new formation with *Wehrmacht* soldiers (no *Waffen-SS*) from the communications zone likewise did not result in a unit fit for action. Also, these members "disappeared" within a few days. Already as of 5 February 1945, the battalion was deployed as infantry and suffered great losses.

On 10 March 1945, the *SS-Pionier-Bataillon 32* was reinforced by the remainder of the *Kampfgruppe* Frenken. This *Pionierkampfgruppe* Frenken (formed from the *SS-Pionier-Ersatz und Ausbildungsregiment Dresden* and consisting of three companies) had thus far been deployed as a *Korpstruppe*. Hereby, the *Kampfgruppenführer SS-Hauptsturmführer* Frenken also took over the command of the *SS-Pionier-Bataillon 32*.

SS-Panzer-Jäger-Abteilung 32

The *Panzerjäger-Kompanie* of the *SS-Regiment* Schill—the former *Gruppe* Rössner (two *Sturmgeschütz-Batterien*) of the *SS-Sturmgeschütz-Schule* at the Bukovany/Bohemia SS military training area—became the foundation of the *SS-Panzer-Jäger-Abteilung 32*.

The *SS-Panzer-Jäger-Abteilung 16*, which originally belonged to the *16. SS-Panzer-Grenadier-Division* "Reichsführer-SS," was likewise used in April 1945 as a replacement for the *SS-Panzer-Jäger-Abteilung 32*.

According to a report from the *Oberkommando der Heeresgruppe* Weichsel, on 7 April 1945, the *32. SS-Division* had 22 *Sturmgeschütze III* and 9 *Sturmhaubitzen 42*. Following the second type of organization of the *Infanterie-Division 44*, the *Infanterie-Division 45* had a requirement of 14 *Sturmgeschütze*—which displays a substantially higher actual number of these weapons.

SS-Flak-Abteilung 32[5]

This detachment developed from the "*Abteilung z.b.V.*" of the *SS-Führungshauptamt*, which was formed at the end of 1944 in the *SS-Flak-Ausbildungs und Ersatzregiment* in Munich/Freimann. On 31 January 1945, they were transferred via railway transport from Munich over Trebbin-Zossen-Fürstenwalde to the Bad Saarow region on the Oder Front.

At the beginning of March 1945 the *Flak-Abteilung z.b.V.* was placed under the command of the *V. SS-Gebirgs-Korps* and went by the name "*SS-Flak-Abteilung 550.*" The transfer to the Front section Brieskow-Pohlitz-Ziltendorf-Oder-Spree-Canal by Fürstenberg followed. The *1. Batterie* took position by Rießen, the *2. Batterie* in Brieskow, and the *3. Batterie* at the bridge between Pohlitz and Ziltendorf. In mid-March 1945 the detachment was placed under the command of the *32. SS-Division "30. Januar"* by order of the *V. SS-Gebirgskorps*.

SS-Nachrichten-Abteilung 32

The transfers from the SS-Nachrichten-Ersatz-Abteilung Eichstädt formed this detachment.

SS-Füsilier-Bataillon 32

In 1944 the *Waffen-SS* school of music in Braunschweig was transferred to Bad Saarow due to increasing air attacks. There it dissolved in January/February 1945, and from these members the *SS-Füsilier-Bataillon 32* was formed in February/March 1945.

SS-Feld-Ersatz-Bataillon 32

The division's own formation for the initially nearly daily, newly arriving assignments.

SS-Sanitätskompanie

It was formed by transfers from the *SS-Sanitäts-Ersatz-Bataillon Stettin*, the *SS-Ärzte-Akademie Graz*, the *SS-Lazarett Prag*, and the *SS-Korps-Sanitäts-Abteilung 505*.

SS-Veterinärkompanie

Formed from the *SS-Veterinär-Ausbildungs-Abteilung* and *Ersatz-Abteilung Wandern*.

Bäckerei-Kompanie and *Schlachterei-Kompanie*

Formed on 30 March 1945, by German personnel from the disbanded 21. *SS-Division* "Skanderbeg."

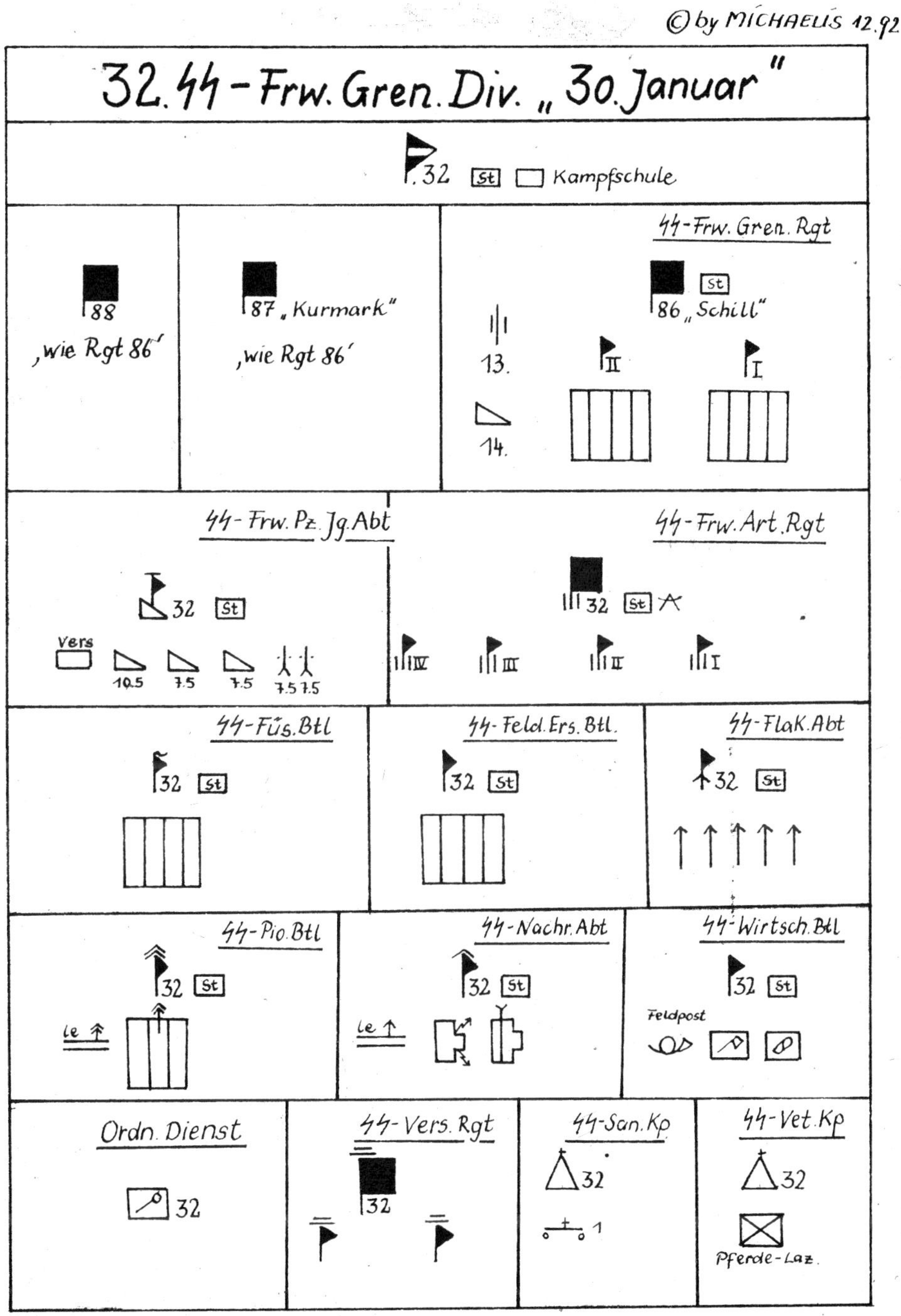
© by MICHAELIS 12.92
32. SS-Frw. Gren. Div. „30. Januar"
32
St
Kampfschule
88
‚wie Rgt 86'
87 „Kurmark"
‚wie Rgt 86'
SS-Frw. Gren. Rgt
St
86 „Schill"
13.
14.
II
I
SS- Frw. Pz. Jg. Abt
32
St
Vers
10.5
7.5
7.5
7.5 7.5
SS-Frw. Art. Rgt
32
St
IV
III
II
I
SS-Füs. Btl
32
St
SS-Feld. Ers. Btl.
32
St
SS-FlaK. Abt
32
St
SS-Pio. Btl
32
St
le
SS-Nachr. Abt
32
St
le
SS-Wirtsch. Btl
32
St
Feldpost
Ordn. Dienst
32
SS-Vers. Rgt
32
SS-San. Kp
32
1
SS-Vet. Kp
32
Pferde-Laz.

Günther Anhalt was born on 23 January 1906, in Breslau [today Wrocław in Poland]. Until July 1943 he was initially *Zugführer*, then *Kompaniechef*, and *Bataillonskommandeur* in the *Leibstandarte-SS* Adolf Hitler. After he took over a battalion in the *SS-Polizei-Regiment 2* in summer 1943, he became *Kommandeur* of this regiment in September 1943. On 12 August 1944, he was awarded with the Knight's Cross to the Iron Cross. From 26 January until approximately 15 February 1945, he led the SS-*Regiment* Kurmark as *SS-Standartenführer* (sp. 87).

Eberhard Baumgart was born on 29 April 1925. After being severely injured in the *3./Panzer-Aufklärungs-Abteilung* of the *Leibstandarte-SS* Adolf Hitler, he was deployed to the *Vorführkompanie* of the *SS-Panz.-Aufkl.-Ers. und Ausb.Abteilung* in the Staumühle camp. From there he voluntarily reported to the *SS-Division "30. Januar"* at the beginning of February 1945.

4

Replacement Supply and Assignments

Replacements came to the *SS-Feldersatz-Bataillon 32* regularly until April 1945 from nearly all SS training and replacement units, the SS schools, from the *Luftwaffe*, the *Marine*, and *Wachmannschaften* of the dissolved KL. From there the enlisted personnel were sent to single units according to need and demand.

Initially other units (for example, *Flak-Abteilung 1204* (RAD), *SS-Kompanie* Heyer (formerly *2./SS-Panzergrenadier-Ausbildungs und Ersatzbataillon 3*)) were placed under the command of the *Division "30. Januar." Kampfgruppen* that were directly under the command of the *V. SS-Gebirgs-Korps* or the *9. Armee* were often involved.

Many small units existed for only a few days, and were either disbanded, split up, or completely withdrew from the area.

The former *SS-Rottenführer* Eberhard Baumgart recalls his path to the division:[6]

*"A February evening in the Staumühle camp in 1945 (*SS-Panzer-Aufklärungs-Ausbildungs-u. Ersatzabteilung*). I am in the* Genesenden-Kompanie *and wait impatiently to go back to my old unit, the* Leibstandarte. *But I'm still not fit for assignment on the front because of my last injury and voluntarily render service in a* Vorführkompanie. *The barrack-room inspection has been over for some time, the lights out. In the iron oven in the middle of the halved barracks, a 'soldier room,' that surrounds twenty bunk beds, the remainder*

of the daily coal ration burns out. Many are already snoring, some are still whispering to each other. In the stifling silence there is suddenly a whistle and shout: 'Out of the beds, you bastards! Go immediately to the teaching barracks! Chop! Chop!' Clatter set in. Quickly through the snow to the ordered assembly room. In semi-darkness – softly lit due to poor darkening equipment – comrades crowding together. Stern commanders interrupt any confusion or thoughts. There is bustle while lining up. Report to the Kompanieführer. *'Men! The Russians have advanced over the ice of the Oder and have formed a bridgehead. Not even fifty kilometers before our Reich's capitol.*

Comrades, men! For this situation the Führer *has ordered the formation of a new* SS-Division, *the* Division '30. Januar.' *I know that neither myself nor any one else can issue the order for combat mission. In this critical situation I can only appeal to your soldierly conscience. It is for the Reich, the* Führer, *Berlin, the final victory – the final battle. For this new and young* SS-Division *the* Führer *needs mature, experienced, battle-tested soldiers. I know that you are these soldiers! You know this yourselves! I appeal to you, follow the call of the* Führer *and voluntarily step forward. At ease!' The first forms broke away from the crowd that was standing in semi-darkness. In the same moment it was as though a dam had come crashing down. Everything moved forward. At least it seemed so. 'I expected nothing less!' the voice of the* Obersturmführer *reported, and let everyone step up before there could be any questions, inquiries or thoughts. During the night weapons, exclusively carbines, in addition, munitions, marching rations and field kits, were received. Shortly before dawn we're sitting on trucks, roll through the Staumühle gate, leave the lousy camp environment behind us and after some time arrive at a goods station. We disappear in live stock wagons. Suddenly, we stop. A murmur of voices grows louder, gets closer, gravel crunching under swift steps. Our wagon door is ripped open. Yelling:* 'Marschkompanie, *step out!' We struggle to our feet. Chaos and confusion. Pushing and shoving. We stand neatly in a row. Then we march into the night, stumble over extensive railway tracks and unexpectedly through a high, arch-shaped wire gate. Left and right deserted-looking stone buildings. We turn into a square that is bordered by the same buildings on one side and gloomy rows of barracks begin to line up behind it. Everything is dead silent. Only the step of our march. Nowhere a guard. No one seems to take notice of our arrival. A frosty chill penetrates through my uniform. Meanwhile we're standing at ease and shift from one foot to the other. The* Führer *have called the* Unterführer *to them. Whispering. A coming and going. A noticeable indecision. Finally, we move into the next best barracks. No locker, no straw mattress. Merely plank-like boards. The knapsack serves as a pillow, coat and cover as bedding. I am shivering. With the first light we are loaded onto truck columns and drive off. Dawn is breaking when we arrive in Rießen. We have to line up at a village square and are briefly informed that the Russians have crossed over the ice of the Oder. The Division* '30. Januar' *is in formation, immediately facing entrenched Russians. It is necessary to close a dangerous breach in the Front and to constrict the Russian bridgehead.*"

It is apparent that this division was a sum of units of the most various origins. The single Front-experienced unit was the *SS-Freiwilligen-Grenadier-Regiment 86* "Schill." In addition to soldiers from schools and *Ersatzeinheiten*, who were at least partially trained and fit for the Front, came "soldiers" without any kind of military training and from the communications zone.

Due to the hasty formation and lack of coordination, it turned out that the division—if considerable success was able to be achieved—was neither fit for attack or defense, or even partially fit for attack, but rather possessed only a meager fitness for defense.

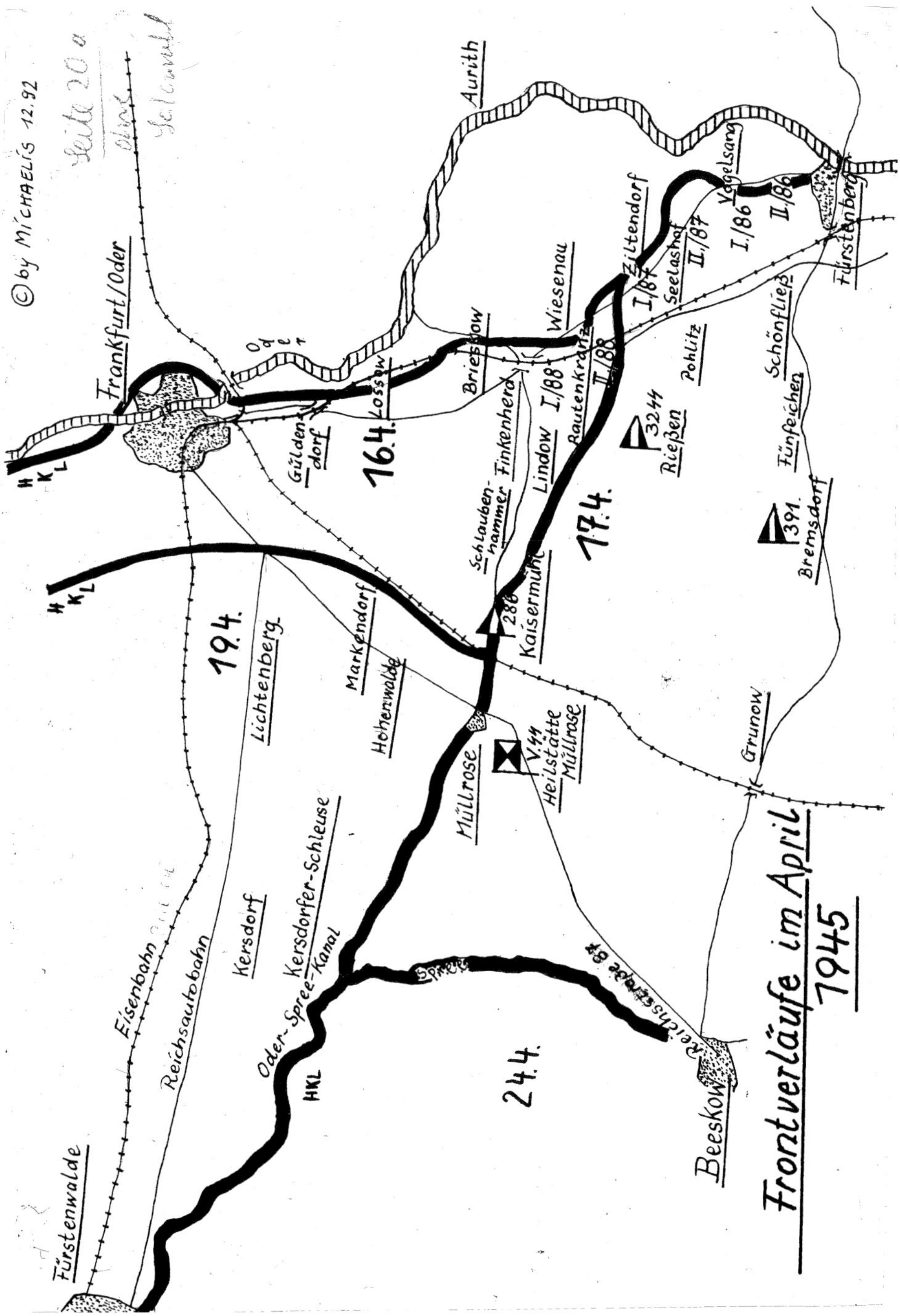
© by Michaelis 12.92
Frankfurt/Oder
Aurith
Oder
HKL
Lossow
Gülden-dorf
16.4.
Brieskow
Finkenherd
Wiesenau
Lindow
I./88
Rautenkranz
II./88
Ziltendorf
I./87
Seelashof
II./87
Vogelsang
I./86
II./86
Fürstenberg
Pohlitz
Schönfließ
3244
Rießen
Fünfeichen
391.
Bremsdorf
17.4.
Schlauben-hammer
Kaisermühl
286
19.4.
Lichtenberg
Markendorf
Hohenwalde
Müllrose
V.44
Heilstätte Müllrose
Grunow
Kersdorfer-Schleuse
Kersdorf
Oder-Spree-Kanal
Eisenbahn
Reichsautobahn
24.4.
Spree
Beeskow
Fürstenwalde
Frontverläufe im April 1945

5

The Division's Assignment Until April 16, 1945[7]

At the end of January 1945 the first *Kampfgruppen* had already set out east of Frankfurt/Oder and south toward Brieskow-Finkenheerd, Siltendorf-Aurith, Vogelsang, and Fürstenberg. These units were not yet under the command of the *SS-Panzer-Grenadier-Division "30. Januar,"* which was at this time in its developmental phase, but rather under the command of the *V. SS-Gebirgs-Korps* of the *391. Sicherungs-Division* (*Generalmajor* Sieckenius). As of 2 February, attack operations were carried out with the objective of crushing the Russian bridgeheads. On 5 and 6 February the first attacks on the Soviet bridgehead by Vogelsang were carried out. Before the evacuation to Friedland, Vogelsang had approximately 600 inhabitants and consisted primarily of single-family homes, several farmsteads, a school, and a church. During the battles for Vogelsang 80% of the town was destroyed. Positions were spread all over town, basements of homes were included (see photographs). Both smoke stacks of a power station south of Vogelsang had an especially negative effect for the Germans during the battles. There were Russian artillery observation points here; it was not just in Vogelsang that each movement could be tracked with Russian artillery fire. On 7 February I./Schill recaptured Vogelsang with *Sturmgeschütze* of the *SS-Panzer-Jäger-Abteilung "30. Januar"* and was afterwards relieved by II./Schill.

On 6 February the *Division "30. Januar"* was supplied with a *Werferbatterie*. The *Batterieführer*, *SS-Untersturmführer* Walter Vahldiek, recalls:[8]

*"First I must establish that with the 30 cm-*Werferbatterie, *which was designated to the '30. Januar' and which I also led, an* Alarmbatterie *was included that was formed on 4 February 1945, in Lübbinchen from the* SS-Werfer-Ausbildungs-Abteilung und Ersatz-Abteilung, *and was supplied to the* '30. Januar' *for the short-term support for resistance assignments on the Oder Front, which was still being built up. The battery consisted of three 30 cm mortars and one 21 cm mortar, and was provided only with a minimum of other weapons and equipment. The mortar crews and* BattrTrupp *divisions were placed primarily with the* 1. (Führerbewerber)/SS-Werfer-Ausb und Ers-Abt, *which after an eight-day mission were already exchanged again for entirely inexperienced crews. Only a meager supply of mortar ammunition (90 rounds) was available, which could be replenished only on one's own initiative. Nevertheless, the battery was already in action on 5 February 1945, and was successfully able to support the resistance combat of the occupying forces of Gut Ziltendorf with the destruction of enemy concentrations and columns. In collaboration with a* Heeres-Artillerie-Abteilung, *objectives in Vogelsang and Russian attacks from Vogelsang continued to be successfully fought. The orders given by* SS-ArtRgtKdr '30. Januar' *partly contradicted the tactics of the mortar weapon and were not feasible. Among other things, the battery was to shoot at and knock over a smoke stack because it had the strongest, and most likely the most effective caliber. The allocated firing position areas would have directly challenged an enemy armed attack after the first volley. Disagreements with the* Artillerie-Kommandeur *with initially unpleasant results were the consequence, in the course of which, however, the stance on the mortar weapon would prevail. Because a continued delivery of munitions could not be counted on after the ammunition, which was provided and procured by the* SS-Werfer-Ers-Abt, *ran out, on 25 February 1945, the*

battery returned to the Ersatz-Abteilung *and was disbanded. During the initial formation of the* '30. Januar' *the battery's only significance was as a stopgap.*"

On 10 February the *Pionier-Bataillon* was deployed as infantry to secure the Oder-Spree Canal south of Wiesenau. On 14 February the German side attempted to destroy the Russian observation point in the power station again. For this, sections of the *Pionier-Bataillon "30. Januar,"* the *Aufklärungszug*/Schill, as well as a platoon from *SS-Kompanie* Heyer were deployed. However, the attack was unsuccessful and completely shattered by the Russians. The result was over 80 fallen soldiers. On 15 February an attack by the *Pionier-Bataillon "30. Januar"* took place in Russian-occupied Wiesenau. This attack was also completely shattered by the Russians' heavy weapons. The *Bataillonskommandeur*, *SS-Hauptsturmführer* König, had fallen in the evening, along with his *Adjutant*, the *Chef der 1. Kompanie*, and half of the battalion.

The situation at the beginning of February 1945 in the Müllrose region is described in a report from the *SS-Obersturmbannführer* Gottmann on 16 February 1945, to the OB of the *Heeresgruppe* Weichsel:[9]

"Assessments of the assignment and the conduct of Wehrmachteinheiten, *as well as the methods of the staff all result in the greatest possible disorganization within the entire Front sector, the* Fronteinheiten *and the* staff *maintain little or no close contact and they are not informed in detail by each other of the facts or the region. For example, in the Front sector companies and battalions deployed to Kienitz-Frankfurt/Oder were often not*

informed of the demarcation of their Front sector as well as of the situation of the person next to them. The Division '30. Januar' *positioned in a sector south of Frankfurt/Oder was not informed for days of the location and approach of the* Anschlußverband *located south.*

The Kampfkommandanten *deployed to single locations for the most part appear uninformed of the situation of the enemy and rely on receiving news on the approach, strength and emergence of enemy forces from stories from stragglers, as well as from the population. Only in a few cases did the opportunity exist, to directly provide information on the enemy situation from* Spähtrupps. *In many cases the observation could be made that the* Kampfkommandanten *were not at all initially waiting for direct enemy action but rather to 'retreat' at the first sight of enemy tanks in close proximity to their defense sector. At the same time this corresponded to the intentions of the* 'Kampfverbände' *previously formed from stragglers....*"

On 25 February 1945, the commanding *General des V. SS-Gebirgs-Korps*, *SS-Obergruppenführer* and *General der Polizei und Waffen-SS* Jeckeln drew up a statement to the reproaches of *SS-Obersturmbannführer* Gottmann. It was clear that these contemporary military reports and documents were full of propaganda:[10]

"*... The reproach that the 32. SS-Freiwilligen-Division '30. Januar' was uninformed for days concerning the location and approach of the* Anschlußverband *located south can initially be repudiated because the division, for lack of a* Divisionskommandeur, *was placed under the command of the right neighboring formation, the* 391. Sicherungs-Division. *The Ia of the* 32. SS-Division *is of the opinion that* SS-Obersturmbannführer *Gottmann presumably got this impression from the lowest units that even in the best circumstances are mostly uninformed of neighboring formations. At any rate, the reporter did not appear at the command post of the* 32. SS-Division...

The discernible atmosphere of panic and apathy in the first days after the Russian invasion has fundamentally changed. The newly formed units have come to know each other. The proper support and not least the criminal conduct of the Russians in the occupied regions, especially toward German women, have strengthened their will to fight."

After the conclusion of the first phase of development, while several *Kampfgruppen* were already destroyed, in mid-February 1945 the *Division "30. Januar"* stood at a Front sector (approximately 25 km) with the following units in close contact with:

Vogelsang/Fürstenberg Bridgehead with: *SS-Panzer-Grenadier-Regiment* "Schill," *I./ Artillerie-Regiment "30. Januar," SS-Kompanie* Heyer,

Ziltendorf/Aurith/Wiesenau Bridgehead with: *SS-Panzer-Grenadier Regiment* "Kurmark," *Pionier-Bataillon "30. Januar," Teile II. und III./Artillerie-Regiment "30. Januar,"*

Bridgehead north of Brieskow/Lossow/Güldendorf with: *Btl.* Hengstmann, *Teile II./ Artillerie-Regiment "30. Januar," Kampfgruppe* Becker (not yet with the *Division "30. Januar"*).

While the bridgeheads could not be destroyed because of the Russian superiority, it was attempted to at least stabilize the Front line. The continued formation and development of the division, which received their own Front sector at the end of February 1945, was carried out. This ran from the northern edge of Fürstenberg to the southern border of Güldendorf.

On 2 March Vogelsang had to be evacuated again by three-fourths. Two days later, at 0700 hours a German attack on Vogelsang began, after which a second followed at 1300 hours. They were carried out by sections of the *Regiment* "Schill" and the *4./SS-Panzer-Jäger-Abteilung "30. Januar"* under its chief, *SS-Hauptsturmführer* Krauß. The attempts to recapture the town failed with an enormous loss of approximately 70 fallen soldiers.

On 11 March there was an attempt to take over the power station, whereby the attack, like before, was unable to evolve and smashed by Soviet artillery. This attack also cost the German side over 70 fallen soldiers!

The *SS-Untersturmführer* at the time, Jochen Polle (Pionierzug/86, 13./86), recalls:[18]

"*Initially, my platoon was with* Regiment *'Schill.' After the Slovakia assignment we remained only a small, pathetic group in Vogelsang. In my absence my proud* Pionierzug *was completely worn out from infantry action. I was then* Bataillons-Adjutant *and later* Führer *of the* 13. Kompanie/86 *in Mixdorf (deployment) before I received my transfer to the* Pionier-Schule. *As an assigned* Stoßtruppführer *in the assault on the power station I had given warning as to the poor preparations. As a result I was relieved, and the* Stoßtrupp *operation was a complete and unnecessary flop. Because of this idiotic order many comrades, also those who participated in the entire war, lost their lives at the last minute.*"

By order of the *9. Armee* on 12 April 1945, the *32. SS-Freiwilligen-Division "30. Januar"* transferred as army reserves as of 18 April 1945, to the region of the *XI. SS-Armee-Korps* (Seelow Heights). In addition, the *SS-Frw.-Gren.-Rgt. 88* was pulled out of position at Brieskow-Finkenheerd on 14 April 1945, and was relieved by sections of the *Grenadier-Regiment 1257* and the *Volkssturm*.

The former *SS-Obersturmführer* and *Kompanieführer* 13./88 recalls:[19]

"Regiment Becker was pulled from the Front around 14 April 1945, in order to stay on standby as reserves in the Müllrose region. A Fahnenjunker-Regiment of the Army took over the sector. Already one or two days later we were ordered back again in a quick march to the same sector.

North of Wiesenau—at the end of our trench in a young small spruce forest west of a ditch—the Russians had invaded our trenches that were occupied by the Fahnenjunker. *In close combat with flamethrowers and hand grenades, we attempted to push them out again. We did not completely succeed. They remained on the eastward slope, and from this flank could fire on our trench position. I was in the trench for reconnaissance, in order to have some effect with my heavy mortars. It was very difficult, because fire control in the small forest was not possible. The Russians were faced from only 50 steps away. We had extremely heavy loses there. Until 14 April a* Bataillon Volkssturm *was placed under our command. The 'old gentlemen' were spread out into the groups. Always two to three men per group.* SS-Obersturmführer *Fischer led the first company in the northernmost section of the* Regiment 88 *and during these days had a nervous breakdown, so I temporarily led this company.*"

In mid-April the *V. SS-Gebirgskorps* transferred the assignment of securing the marching route for the soldiers of the "Festung Frankfurt/Oder" to the *Division "30. Januar."* Firstly, this was to happen over the Kersdorfer Schleuse to Fürstenwalde; secondly, toward the southwest over Buschmühlen-Brücke – Neubrück to Beeskow. For this purpose, for both of these "escape routes," two *Kampfgruppen* were formed from the *32. SS-Division*:

1) *Kampfgruppe* Krauß (*Chief 4./SS-Panzer-Jäger-Abteilung 32*):

2. und 4. Kp./SS-Pz.Jg.Abt. 32, a *Kp./SS-Pio.Btl. 32*, a *Btl. Festungsgrenadiere* (*Army*), and a *Füsilierkompanie* of the Army. The task was primarily the securing of the Reichsautobahn to Berlin.

2) *Kampfgruppe* Schöttle (*Chief 1./SS-Pz.Jg.Abt. 32*):

1. und 3. Kp./SS-Pz.Jg.Abt. 32, a *Kp./SS-Pio.Btl. 32*, a *Zug Panzerzerstörer* of the 14./86, and a *Kp./Füs.Btl. 32*

On 12 and 13 April 1945, the *III./SS-A.R.32* supported the failed attempt of the *600. Infanterie-Division* (*Russ. Nr. 1*) to smash the Soviet bridgehead south of Fürstenberg.

As of the morning of 14 April the Soviets proceeded with artillery into the sector of the *286. Infanterie-Division* and the *32. SS-Division*. Shortly thereafter, six battalion-strong Russian attacks from the Aurith bridgehead were carried out with the objective of obtaining a better line of departure for their major offensive on 16 April 1945. The main battle line at Vogelsang-Ziltendorf could thereby be maintained, while an invasion took place by the *SS-Regiment 87*. This could finally be sealed off, and in doing so a Russian assault gun was destroyed.

SS-Junker at the time, Günter Adam, was transferred on 15 April 1945, to the *32. SS-Division*:[12]

"*I reached the division's command post in Rieβen, where I was already expected and informed of my new unit: the* 13. Kompanie, Regiment 86. *I became* Zugführer *of the* I. Zug *(light infantry artillery). The enlisted personnel —partly very young, partly older, many inexperienced at war—otherwise made a good impression. The previous* Zugführer, *an* Unterscharführer, *became* Stellungsunterführer, *my deputy, and from then on there were no difficulties. Armament and equipment were good (Vehicles, Eintonnerzugmaschinen - half-track vehicles). Only a few grenades were available and were only permitted to be fired on command. The positions of the artillery were well developed and camouflaged. The* Unterscharführer *was an expert. The observation point, approximately 500-600 m farther ahead, was located in well-planned trenches, but was to be used carefully.*

The Russians were only 70 m away at the time. An uncomfortable situation. Because firing was not permitted we had time, and I acquainted myself with my comrades, the Zugführer *of the* II. Zug, *likewise a young* Oberscharführer *with extensive IG experience. According to the mood of the troop, we would stop here and 'sideslip' the Russians; particularly as a speech from* General *Busse was announced to the groups: 'Soldiers on the Eastern Front, hold out for two more days, you will be able and will also do so, then that is it. Greetings from your* General *Busse!' Enormous cheer broke out, as it could mean that now the wonder weapons were available as promised.*"

Günter Adam was born on 29 June 1923, in Ruß (Klaipėda Region). On 1 June 1940, he joined the *Inf.Geschütz-Ersatz-Bataillon* "Germania." After being injured in the *SS-Regiment* "Westland," he came to the *9. SS-Panzerdivision* "Hohenstaufen." On 5 January 1945, he was appointed *SS-Junker*, and a mission followed as *KpFhr* with the *545. Volksgrenadier-Division*. From there he transferred to the *32. SS-Division* on 15 April 1945.

The following photographs display the town's entrance sign and the positions in Vogelsang.

6

The Soviet Major Offensive on April 16, 1945[11]

On Monday, 16 April 1945, it had come thus far; the finale began.

At 0300 hours in the morning the Russian air force flew the first attacks against the German positions. When the last wave of Soviet bombers released their charges, at 0500 hours a barrage from several thousand artillery began on the German assembly and defense areas. One hour later, on a 400 km stretch of the Front, the last assault began. Two main focal points emerged in the first hours for the *9. Armee*. One was Frankfurt/Oder, which with Altdamm/Stettin [today Dąbie/Szczecin in Poland] formed the single German bridgeheads on the eastern Oder shore. The other was the battle area at the Seelow Heights. The "Festung Frankfurt" was able to hold off all attacks, and also at Seelow the German soldiers, even initially suffering heavy losses, could maintain their positions.

The Russian 33rd Army (8th, 49th, 64th, 89th, 119th, 222nd, 323rd, 362nd, and 383rd Rifle Division) under General Zwetajew attacked the *V. SS-Gebirgskorps*. In close combat, the *SS-Regiment 87* was able to resolve the matter of an enemy invasion northwest of Wiesenau. An invasion by Güldendorf towards the west by the *Fahnenjunker-Regiment 1257* and *Volkssturm* necessitated the mission of the *SS-Regiment 88*, on standby as *Eingreifreserve* somewhat north. This could only briefly take the former positions again, and was overrun a short time later. The *I./88* was completely crushed, while the II./88 formed a new line of defense by Ober-Lindow.

The *SS-Obersturmführer* H. Sch. (*KpChef 13./88*)[20] reported:

"After the Russian invasion they initially stopped on the western edge of Oberlindow. We were in Schlaubehammer with the Regimentsstab. *The Russians attempted to go around Schlaubehammer in a pincer movement through Brieskower Heide and Lindower Heide.*

My company was situated on the northernmost eastern edge of Schlaubehammer. In this direction I secured and, during a Spähtrupp *operation, was able to capture Russian artillery (approximately 15 cm) that was loaded with a shrapnel cartridge (rusty waste iron). After heavy firing – particularly in the northern region of Schlaubehammer –we set off to the edge of the town Müllrose through 'Stalinorgeln.' Several days later we proceeded from there, toward the southwest on a good road."*

A Russian attack southwest of Wiesenau toward Rießen was sealed off by sections of the *SS-Feldersatz-Bataillon 32*, the *SS-Pionier-Bataillon 32*, and the *I./SS-A.R. 32*.

On 16 April 1945, the following order of the day from the "*Führer*" was announced to all soldiers on the Eastern Front. The manner of expression, entreaties, and promises—from which nothing happened—clearly displayed the despair of the "greatest warlord of all time":

"Soldiers of the German Eastern Front!

The Jewish-Bolshevist mortal enemy with its masses has come forward to attack for the last time. He attempts to shatter Germany into pieces and wipe out our people. You soldiers in the East know well what fate threatens the German women, girls and children. While the old men and children are being murdered, women and girls are degraded as barracks whores. The rest march to Siberia.

We have foreseen this strike, and since January everything has taken place to develop a strong front. The enemy will be received by powerful artillery.

The losses of our infantry have been replenished by numerous new units. Alarmeinheiten, *new formations and* Volkssturm *reinforce our front.*

This time the Bolshevik will experience Asia's old fate, that is, he must and will bleed to death before the capital of the German Reich.

Whoever does not fulfill his duty at this time will be treated as a traitor to our people.

The regiment or division that would leave their position would behave so shamefully and feel disgrace before the women and children who withstand terror bombing in our cities.

Pay attention most of all to the traitorous few officers and soldiers who, in order to protect their pitiful lives, fight against us in Russian employ, maybe even in German uniform. Whoever gives the order to retreat, is to be immediately arrested and if necessary killed that moment, no matter what rank or without even knowing him.

Berlin will remain German, Vienna will be German again, and Europe will never become Russian.

Form a sworn community for the defense, not for the empty notion of a Fatherland, but rather for the defense of your home, your women, your children and also our future.

In these hours the entire German people are watching you, my 'eastern fighters,' and are hoping that because of your steadfastness, your fanaticism, your weapons and your leadership, the Bolshevik onslaught will suffocate in a bloodbath.

During the moment, in which fate removes the greatest war criminals of all time from this earth, the turn of the war will be the judge.

Signed, Adolf Hitler"

The *Divisionskommandeur*, *SS-Standartenführer* Kempin, added, without mentioning the final victory, but rather the final stage of the war:

"*SS-Männer!*

In the final stage of this war the Führer *has spoken to the Eastern Front.*

As National Socialists we bear the proud name: Division "30. Januar."

As political soldiers we realize the objectives of Bolshevism.

Whatever may happen, we stand here and defend the substance of our people with our own SS-Männer *energy and tenacity.*

Germany will and must live, we will not let the hideous face of brutish Bolshevism leave its mark on it.

From this our slogan: Dig, take cover, and kill!

Long live our glorious people!

Long live the Führer*!*"

During the night of 16 April, the Russians reached Rautenkranz by crossing over the Oder-Spree Canal. The *I./SS-Feldersatz-Bataillon 32* set out from Rießen, and for a short time was able to reoccupy the line to the canal. The *I./87* located north of Ziltendorf had to move back over the Oder-Spree Canal due to enemy force. The *SS-Feldersatz-Bataillon 32*, the *SS-Flak-Abteilung 32*, and the *Fahnenjunker-Regiment 1257* moved into new sectors. The *I./SS-A.R. 32* had moved into positions at Pohlitz – Schönfließ [today Trzcińsko-Zdrój in Poland], the *II. Abteilung* south of Lindow, and the *IV. Abteilung* at Hohenwalde.

On 18 April the remainder of the II./88, practically destroyed after the last battles, moved back to Kaisermühl and stood ground until 21 April in the evening. On 18 April, east of Markendorf, *Kampfgruppe* Krauß was in various battles. At 1000 hours in the morning *Kampfgruppe* Frenken, formed by sections of the *SS-Pionier-Bataillon 32* and the *SS-Feld-Ersatz-Bataillon 32*, as well as the *SS-Panzerjäger-Abteilung 32*, attacked the Russian troops that crossed the Oder-Spree Canal west of Rautenkranz. When the units neared the canal, they were stopped by Soviet infantry fire from the other, elevated side of the shore. In return, new Russian troops crossed the canal. Shortly beforehand, another German attack was to be carried out at 1500 hours, but the Russians took the initiative and attacked with heavy infantry forces. *Kampfgruppe* Frenken was forced to retreat.

On 19 April sections of the *32. SS-Division* situated at the main battle line (HKL) were able to maintain the Lichtenberg - Markendorf line and strengthen it north of Rießen-Rautenkranz. The Russian attack that was carried out from Rautenkranz by the *Kampfgruppe* Frenken was able to be sealed off. The *XI. SS-Armee-Korps* that was hard-pressed by the Soviet invasion at Seelow urgently requested the *32. SS-Freiwilligen-Grenadier-Division,* which was planned to be used as an army reserve. After the *Ablöse-Division* still had not arrived, two *Regimentskampfgruppen* were formed. One consisted of the *Stab 86*, *II./86* and *II./87*, and on 20 and 21 April set out to the *XI. SS-Armeekorps* in the Fürstenwalde region along the Spree to Müggelsee. For a while the regiment command post was located in Tannengrün.

The *SS-Junker* Günter Adam also belonged to the *Kampfgruppe* 86:

"*Everywhere around us there's rumbling, only here is it calm. Something is happening. But then we receive the order to pull out. The Russians have broken through in two locations. Our artillery are limbered up, and the entire platoon must find a spot on the two tractors. Also, our* II. Zug *is already there, and we await our orders, as the Russians set a curtain fire behind a small pinewood that is shielding us. The forest is immediately on fire. Our* Kompanieführer *wants to go through this inferno with the tractors. But because hardly anything can be recognized in the smoke, I tell him it does not serve any purpose. The vehicles are stuck, and no one can make it through. Also, my comrade from the* II.

Zug *agrees with me, we want to wait and see what happens as soon as the fire has died down. He calls us cowards and storms into the burning forest. We can't hold him back. We take cover, and soon the Russians' fire subsides. The forest fire has calmed, and it becomes lighter and there is more visibility. I go somewhat deeper into the forest and find our* Kompanieführer. *He is dead. We drive off and make contact with other sections of the* Kampfgruppe. *Around evening we reach Fürstenwalde. There must have been fighting here already, because everywhere there are traces of action...*"

The second *Regimentskampfgruppe*, which was to hold the old HKL until the arrival of *Ablöseeinheiten*, was formed from the staff of the *SS-Regiment 87*, the *I./86* and *I./87*, and had to hold the approximately 20 km long Front of Ziltendorf-Vogelsang alone, which meant that approximately 20 soldiers had to secure one kilometer.

On 21 April Russian tank formations passed through Spreewald, cavalry troops advanced over the Lübben-Halbe railway line, and *Schützenrudel* infiltrated the narrows between Teupitz and Königs-Wusterhausen. Lichtenberg and Erkner were lost after heavy battles, and the Russian troops reached the eastern shore of the Müggelsee. On 22 April *Kampfgruppe 86* reached Dannenreich with a battalion and formed a new battle line by Neu-Zittau. *Kampfgruppe* Krauß fought near Wernsdorf, while the Soviets crossed the Spree in several places, unable to be stopped. At midday the Russian troops already stood before Wernsdorf, which was defended by the *II./86* (*Kampfgruppe 86*), and took the area under mortar fire. The Russian objective was Niederlehme. As a result, *Kampfgruppe* Krauß pulled back to Königs-Wusterhausen.

On 22 April, the first units of the 1st Belarusian Front and the 1st Ukrainian Front arrived at Müggelsee and encircled the *XI. SS-Armeekorps*, *V. SS-Gebirgskorps*, and *V. Armeekorps* in the region of Guben – Müllrose – Fürstenwalde – Königs-Wusterhausen and Lübben. The *9. Armee* was trapped.

Units of the Soviet 52nd Army came from the south, from the west units of the 28th Army, from the north sections of the 3rd and 69th Army, and from the east formations of the 33rd Army.

On 23 April the *Oberkommando* of the army permitted an invasion of the pocket toward the northwest to the *12. Armee*. Together with them, the *9. Armee* was to relieve Berlin. On the morning of 23 April 1945, the positions on the Oder were given over by the *Regimentskampfgruppe 87* to *Volkssturmverbände* from Thuringia and army units. Half an hour later the Russians were already in these positions. The *Kampfgruppe* returned to the Spree line on both sides of Beeskow, and from there marched over Storkow and Friederdorf to Prieros. After a failed breakthrough attempt by Erkner toward the Reich's Capital Berlin on 24 April (!), the *Regimentsgruppe 86* was annihilated along the Oder-Spree Canal line and Spree. The *II./87* was nearly completely shattered during blocking missions along the Spree and the canal. The *II./86* went down in Wernsdorf. The occupying troops of the "Festung Frankfurt/Oder" were also finally permitted to retreat toward the west due to the hopeless situation. On 24 April the Eastern Front ran from Fürstenwalde over Beeskow to east of Lübbenau, and the *I./SS-Pionier-Bataillon 32* stood together with sections of the *SS-FEB 32* by Ahrensdorf-Behrensdorf, south of Saarow, in heavy resistance combat.

On 25 April the remainder of the shattered *Division "30. Januar"* assembled in Gräbendorf. Along with the soldiers were thousands of civilians with the last of their belongings; in addition to small suitcases and handcarts, ox-drawn carriages stood in the forests.

Afterwards the situation was barely comprehensible, because there was hardly any more reconnaissance from the German side, so no one knew exactly where the Russians were located. Not until contact with the enemy did one realize that the Soviet soldiers had already infiltrated the forests. Together with other units and refugees the remainder of *"30. Januar"* moved toward Hermsdorf on forest roads. Here an attempt was made to form a blocking line once more and keep the Soviets from Hermsdorf. But on the evening of 27 April, the Russians were also able to invade this town.

Soldiers as well as civilians fled toward Märkisch-Buchholz. The town of Hermsdorf was able to be reclaimed once more for a short time by units of *"30. Januar"*—the 700 wounded of the *9. Armee* were left behind there with medical accompaniment.

7

Halbe[13]

From Märkisch-Buchholz the encircled troops moved to "Forsthaus Hammer." There existed absolutely no order any longer, or superior command. The units were scattered, and single solders from various divisions and regiments were found together in small groups. As of this point, there was no longer any concrete assignment reconstructed for the shattered *32. SS-Freiwilligen-Grenadier-Division "30. Januar."*

The common goal was to reach the *12. Armee*. "Forsthaus Hammer" became the combat post of the encircled *9. Armee*. The pocket had a size of approximately 15 km^2. On 28 April 1945, around 1400 hours *General* Busse conducted a briefing, after which at 1800 hours an attempt at escaping toward the west was to be carried out. For this purpose, the commanding *General V. SS-Gebirgskorps*, Friedrich Jeckeln, ordered to destroy all heavy weapons and equipment! Nothing was to be left over to the Soviets in a useable condition. The process was assigned to the commanding *General der Waffen-SS* Kleinheisterkamp. He formed two spearheads that were to breach the Soviet block at Halbe and allow for the escape of soldiers and civilians toward the west. The task to cover the escape to the east was assigned to the *32. SS-Division*. The spearheads were primarily formed from the remainder of the *Panzer-Abteilung* "Kurmark," the *SS-Panzer-Aufklärungs-Abteilung 10* and the *SS-Panzer-Abteilung 502*. *SS-Obergruppenführer* Kleinheisterkamp, who presumably decided to commit suicide during the night of 29/30 April during the breakthrough to the *12. Armee*, left the groups of soldiers who were standing at the edge of the forest and

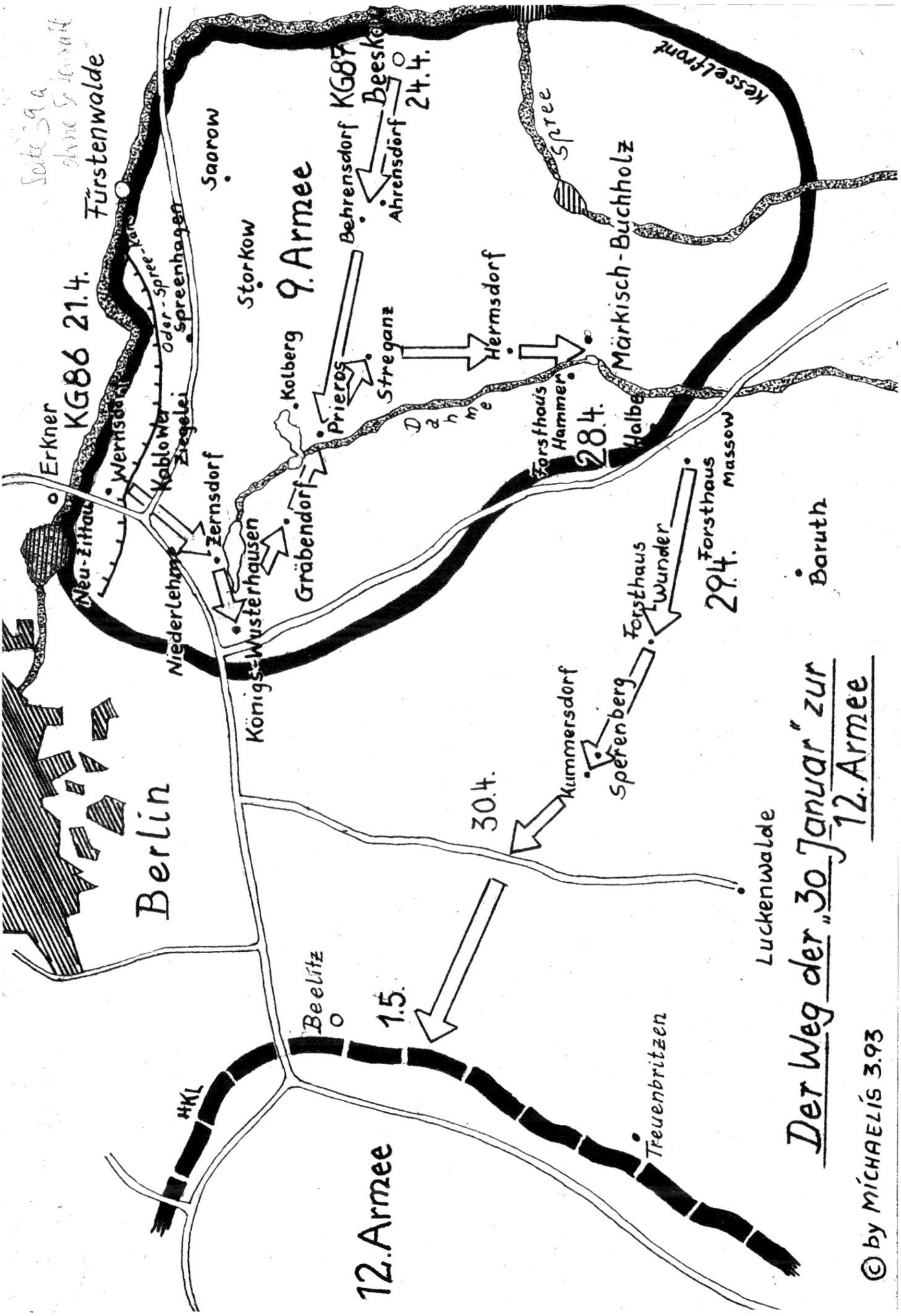
Berlin
Erkner
KG86 21.4.
Fürstenwalde
Neu-Zittau
Wernsdorf
Kablow
Ziegelei
Oder-Spree-Kanal
Spreenhagen
Saarow
Storkow
9. Armee
Behrensdorf
KG87
Beeskow
Ahrensdorf
24.4.
Kesselfront
Spree
Märkisch-Buchholz
Hermsdorf
Kolberg
Prieros
Streganz
Dahme
Forsthaus Hammer
28.4.
Halbe
Zernsdorf
Niederlehme
Königs-Wusterhausen
Gräbendorf
Forsthaus Massow
Forsthaus Wunder
29.4.
Baruth
Forsthaus
Sperenberg
Kummersdorf
30.4.
Luckenwalde
Beelitz
1.5.
Treuenbritzen
HKL
12. Armee
Der Weg der „30 Januar" zur 12. Armee
© by MICHAELIS 3.93

called out, "Freedom." At 1800 hours artillery preparation followed with the last available artillery. After there was no more ammunition, the artillery was destroyed. At 1830 hours the tanks of the spearheads lined up. An hour later the spearheads stood before Halbe. Without encountering decisive resistance, the *Panzerspitzen* entered the town, until they were forced to stop at a tank trap on the main street. Here, all at once, heavy Russian resistance fire (Pak, mortar, artillery) began, upon which panic immediately spread. The people had experienced so much in the last days that their nerves were shot. During this armed attack the vehicles became disabled—several were left totally destroyed and could not be cleared out. While many tried to go around Halbe, the majority continued to move into Halbe as if in a trance. The town portrayed an image of horror. Every which way, next to civilians there were dead Russian and German soldiers. All possible objects from baby carriages to trunks were scattered on the streets.

While the first groups at Halbe fought their way through to the west, sections of the *32. SS-Division* still north were engaged in heavy rearguard action with advancing Russians. On 28 April the remainder of the *I./86* led a last successful counterattack in the Hermsdorf-Streganz region "with blanks." Afterwards the battalion was split into two sections, whereby one group was destroyed in a low-flying Soviet aircraft attack and the other was able to struggle through to Beelitz.

The *SS-Rottenführer* Eberhard Baumgart was in the *Divisionssicherungskompanie "30. Januar"* during the breakthrough attempt and was severely injured at Halbe:[14]

"Night falls. All around the dark forest movement is perceptible. Time elapses. Nothing happens, except that we 15 Rottenführer *and* Sturmmänner, *who should actually be sitting on the tanks, are being sent back to the assembled company. I suppose, that the gentlemen from the staff would themselves like to drive along. A little later the company sets off. Sandy forest paths wherever you step in the dark. After some time we fan out with the explicit order to pay attention to contact from the sides. We cross over a wide asphalt street, and I read on a road sign that it leads back to Märkisch-Buchholz and forward to Halbe. Russian artillery fire in front of us from the Halbe region. Grenades of all caliber explode in the treetops, snap trunks, tear holes and swirl sod through the air. Springing from cover to cover we see a train station. The roof of the storage shed begins to burn, and in the light from the fire I can read the station sign: Halbe... After just 1,000 meters we near gray colossi. They are tanks, our three tanks: two Tigers and a Panther. I am right. But why are they so close together? I move forward and am suddenly in front of a tank trap. Built solid from two rows of thick pine trunks and likewise solidly sealed and filled with sand. While considering what is to be done, a heavy mortar attack takes place. When this dies down, several officers put their heads together. Something will certainly be done soon. The best thing would be to wait here by the tanks. Suddenly: whistling of bullets, flashing, ringing, pressure, smoke, everything happens at once, my legs are ripped away from underneath*

me, I'm lifted up, twirled around and in the same moment crash onto the torn tar surface of the street. I'm aware of the constant impacts all around, but they no longer make me wince. I am disconnected from reality. Instead I see my mother sitting in the sun, our cherry tree in the garden and the high wooden fence in front of it. Everything seems peaceful. When things are somewhat clear again, I notice that my mouth and lips are full of pieces of gravel. My back is soaking wet and blood is trickling from my legs...."

The *SS-Junker* Günter Adam (Remainder of *Kampfgruppe 86*)[15] recalls:

"*Just at the entrance of Halbe there is some kind of industrial area that is enclosed by a strong wire-netting fence. There is roaring from all sides. Dead among dead, and we rush on. After the streets are covered with hundreds of wounded, dead soldiers and civilians, the tanks simply roll over them. Heavy rifle fire while crossing a street. A terrible impact on my chest – now I'm done, I think, and fall. However, I figure out that nothing has happened to me, but rather my binoculars were shot to pieces. I rest in a house entrance and encounter an old acquaintance from the* Junkerschule Poznań/Treskau. *And again it's "pushing forward," shortly thereafter we have lost sight of each other. Combat rages until I manage with only a few to reach the town. We cannot believe that we have made it....*"

8

The Breakthrough to the *12. Armee*[16]

At dawn on 29 April refugees and soldiers reached the Berlin-Cottbus autobahn, which is located west of Halbe. Although the mood had somewhat improved—they made it, so they thought—everything was still chaotic. Few officers were capable of properly leading soldiers. The first meeting point after Halbe was "Försterei Massow"—west of the autobahn. Endless streams of wounded soldiers came here. In addition to hunger and thirst, the care of the wounded was a main issue that could only be solved by chance.

The next objective was "Försterei Wunder," and again a woeful procession, which still consisted of several thousand people, set out. The distance to the *12. Armee* was estimated to be 60 km—and without fuel or supplies—the only stop was made by the remaining few tanks that took their fuel from trucks and destroyed tanks. During midday on 30 April a Pak blocking line on the Berlin-Luckenwalde street had to be fought down and the fortified village of Kummersdorf taken by storm.

Many staffs, officers, soldiers, and segments of the population found their last resting place in the forests during these days. On 30 April several hundred men of the *32. SS-Freiwilligen-Grenadier-Division "30. Januar"* were again in the Kummersdorf region. Except for few, the majority of the division was either already in Soviet war captivity or had fallen. On this day the *V. Armeekorps* took over the command of the breakthrough after contact to the staff of the *XI. SS-Armeekorps* no longer existed. During the night the AOK 12 reported via radio that the most opportune breakthrough point was located south of Beelitz.

The remainder of the *9. Armee* formed for their last march. In the front was the last *Tiger-Panzer* of the *9. Armee*—behind this, soldiers and civilians stormed the Russian positions with loud, despairing cries of "Hooray." No one looked around anymore to see how many hundreds of people were shot down by Soviet machine guns! On 1 May 1945, the last ones had made it. But with these emaciated and desperate soldiers a relief attack could no longer be carried out on Berlin. The objective was only to get over the Elbe into American war captivity. Approximately 150 men of the *SS-Division "30. Januar"* crossed over the Elbe bridge by Tangermünde and surrendered to the American 102nd Infantry Division. For them the war had finally come to an end.

SS-Obersturmführer H. Sch. (*KpFhr 13/88*):[21]

"*On the way to Beeskow we were constantly fired upon by Russian low-flying aircraft. From there we went toward Storkow to Scharmützelsee. There Becker disbanded the remaining battalion with the words that we were at an end with our military force and don't stand a chance. He gave us the order to try to reach Torgau toward the Elbe. There we would encounter the Americans. From then on, in addition to the rest of my* 13. Kompanie, *a total of approximately 300 men stood under me. Without maps of this area, we marched in a general direction toward the west. I believe we passed Märkisch Buchholz and Baruth until west of Luckenwalde. On this path we often came into contact with fighting. While crossing the autobahn by Halbe/Teupitz there was heavy fire from Russian tanks. Around 3 April 1945, in the Baruth region the rest of my unit disbanded. With such a large crowd it was hopeless getting through. In small groups we attempted to pass north or south of*

Luckenwalde, where the Russians were strongly concentrated. Two kilometers before Luckenwalde I was wounded and came into Russian captivity."

The *SS-Rottenführer* Eberhard Baumgart came into Soviet captivity in the Luckenwalde region:[22]

"*Shouting loudly, earth brown soldiers moved through the undergrowth:* 'Njemetzki Kamerrad. Woina kaput. Na Doma!' *(German comrades. The war is over. Time to go home!) They reach us, laugh with relieved expressions. They throw their submachine guns over their backs, pull out cigarettes. Pass them out. They step toward us injured soldiers and pass around canteens.* 'Na Doma. Woina kaput!' *I breathe and am relieved. The critical moment is over. These soldiers are members of the Ukrainian Front. They escort us jokingly and buckle down when the* Panjewagen *is stuck in deep sand. We drive by camping troops. The Soviet soldiers jump, rush to the column, and amicably wave:* 'Woina kaput!' *Finally we come to a town whose streets and yards are full of soldiers and baggage vehicles. Here the frisking begins.* 'Urri, Urri!' – *and many nice watches are gone...*"

The *SS-Junker* Günter Adam reports on his journey from Kummersdorf to the Elbe:[23]

"The next morning we reach, as was thought, the Kummersdorf region. Everywhere there are recently fallen soldiers, they could have not fallen prior to the previous evening or during the night. An eerie area. But then we encounter a larger troop of Waffen-SS. *At the spearhead is a military utility vehicle,* SS-Brigadeführer *Wagner. There is trust in this man, and we stay with the crowd. We quickly proceed and resistance is overcome. Large clusters of infantrymen, often without weapons, cling to us, but they don't seem to want to fight any more. As soon as guns fire, they disappear.*

In front of Beelitz there is heavy breakthrough combat, whereby several, including myself, lose contact to the main group. We make it and a short time later are in the arms of comrades of the 12. Armee. *We are dead tired, and it is already dark when we reach a wide street. Here within a small perimeter traffic is overwhelming. Not far form us a fully loaded truck stops, and we run toward it. After the loading area is completely occupied, I find a spot on the fender. Initially we head toward Belzig and then on to Burg. When we arrive the next day, they say, 'The* Führer *has fallen!' We cannot or do not want to believe it, but this report is confirmed by all sides. We are stunned, many of us cry, until now we have believed in the* Führer *and hoped for the 'wonder weapons.' Has everything come to an end? The attempt to cross over the Elbe fails, and we head north to Tangermünde. Here we cross over to the Americans..."*

On 9 May 1945, the last *Wehrmachtsbericht* announced:[17]

"*Since midnight the weapons have quieted on all fronts. By order of the* Großadmiral *the* Wehrmacht *has ceased all hopeless combat. With this, the nearly six-year heroic struggle has come to an end. It has brought us great victories as well as great defeats. In the end, the German* Wehrmacht *is honorably inferior to a tremendous superior strength.*

True to his oath, the German soldier has made unforgettable achievements for his people with the utmost commitment. The homeland has supported him to the end with all forces and the greatest sacrifices. The unparalleled achievements on the Front and from the homeland will receive their ultimate appreciation in a later, fair judgment of history.

The opponent will not fail to recognize the achievements and sacrifices of the German soldiers on land, sea and air. Therefore, each soldier can proudly lay down their weapons and in the most difficult hour of our history bravely and confidently work for the eternal life of our people.

In this difficult hour, the Wehrmacht *remembers your comrades who have fallen before the enemy. The dead have sworn unconditional loyalty, obedience and discipline with respect to the Fatherland, which bleeds from countless wounds.*"

9

The Strength and Losses of the *Division "30.Januar"*

After *Kampfgruppen* were established within the first days of the division's formation and were deployed, the strength of the division during this time is difficult to determine. Constant losses were compensated for numerically, with constant replacements that were severely less trained. In February 1945 the losses of the division amounted to: 314 fallen soldiers, 1,385 wounded, and 87 missing. Together 1,786 men.

What has survived is a report on combat strength of the *32. SS-Freiwilligen-Grenadier-Division "30. Januar"* on 17 March 1945. That is, without the *SS-Regiment 88*, which was not incorporated until later, and the *SS-Flak-Abteilung*. On this day the *SS-Division* amounted to a combat strength of 2,846 men. For the *Kampfeinheiten* of the division this yields a strength of approximately 250 men per battalion. If 50 sick and wounded men are again added to each battalion, a ration strength of approximately 6,000 men results for the total existing 16 battalions (including *Versorgungseinheiten*, etc.), and corresponds approximately to the strength of an *Infanterie-Division* according to the model in the abridged "Gliederung III" in 1945, whose actual total strength amounted to approximately 6,300 men for two grenadier regiments to two battalions. The entire *V. SS-Gebirgs-Korps* had a combat strength of 18,769 men at their disposal, whereby half were still situated at the "Festung Frankfurt/Oder."

From the *32. SS-Division*, in March 1945 407 men had fallen, 1,447 were wounded, and 336 missing. Together 2,190 men.

In April 1945 several *Kampfgruppen* were formed from the division, whereby both *Kampfgruppen 86* and *87*, reinforced by the remainder of the shattered units, were able to be used as two grenadier regiments.

The abridged "*Gliederung III*" of the *Infanterie-Division* in 1945 was maintained only approximately. In the month of April circa 4,000 soldiers of the *Division "30. Januar"* had fallen or had come into Soviet war captivity - mostly wounded. Approximately 800 of these were officially reported as missing after the war.

Only few could cross the Elbe and surrender to the Americans.

10

Staffing and Military Postal Service Numbers

SS-Panzer-Grenadier-Division "30. Januar"/32. SS-Freiwilligen-Grenadier-Division "30. Januar"

Divisionsstab

1/26/45-2/5/45	*SS-Standartenführer* Mühlenkamp (mdFb.)
2/5/45-2/17/45	*SS-Standartenführer* Joachim Richter
2/17/45-3/15/45 (?)	*SS-Oberführer* Adolf Ax
3/15/45- 5/45	*SS-Standartenführer* Hans Kempin
(*Adjutant*)	*SS-Sturmbannführer* Lenz
Division Staff:	Military Postal Service Number 05 662

***SS-Freiwilligen-Grenadier-Regiment 86* "Schill"**

	SS-Obersturmbannführer Eccher
(*Adjutant*)	*SS-Hauptsturmführer* Richter
	6. Kompanie
1/1/45-2/7/45	*SS-Untersturmführer* Nikolaus
2/7/45- 5/45	*SS-Obersturmführer* Gollo
(*Stabsscharführer*)	*SS-Hauptscharführer* Bärwald
Staff, 13. and 14. Kp	Military Postal Service Number 26 667 A, B, C
I. Btl. with 1.-4. Kp.	*Military Postal Service Number 33 920*
II. Btl. with 5.-8. Kp.	*Military Postal Service Number 35 520*

SS-***Freiwilligen-Grenadier-Regiment 87*** "Kurmark"

1/25/45-2/15/45 (?)	*SS-Standartenführer* Anhalt
2/15/45- 5/45	*SS-Sturmbannführer* Vollmer
IA	*SS-Hauptsturmführer* Wiesmayer
Ordonnanz-Offizier	*SS-Untersturmführer* Weiz

Pionierzugführer	*SS-Untersturmführer* Hyronimus
Staff, 13. and 14. Kp.	*Military Postal Service Number 07 776 A, B, C*
I. Btl. with 1.-4. Kp.	*Military Postal Service Number 08 964*
II. Btl. with 5.-8. Kp.	*Military Postal Service Number 10 036*

SS-Freiwilligen-Grenadier-Regiment 88

3/45- 5/45	*SS-Sturmbannführer* Becker
Chief 1. Kompanie	*SS-Hauptsturmführer* Fischer
	Military Postal Service Number 38 416

SS-Artillerie-Regiment 32

1/26/45-3/2/45	*SS-Obersturmbannführer* Hufmann
3/2/45-	*SS-Sturmbannführer* Ernst
- 5/45	*SS-Sturmbannführer* Lorenz
Stabscharführer	*SS-Hauptscharführer* Marks
Staff and Stabsbttr.	*Military Postal Service Number 11 586*
I. Abt. with 1. and 2. Bttr.	*Military Postal Service Number 16 881*
II. Abt. with 3. and 4. Bttr.	*Military Postal Service Number 18 539*
III. A. with 5. and 6. Bttr.	*Military Postal Service Number 19 714*
IV. Abt.	*No Military Postal Service Number*

SS-Pionier-Bataillon 32

2/2/45-2/15/45	*SS-Hauptsturmführer* König
2/15/45-2/24/45	*SS-Sturmbannführer* Huditz
2/25/45-3/10/45	*SS-Hauptsturmführer* Schütte
3/11/45- 5/45	*SS-Hauptsturmführer* Frenken
(*Adjutant*)	*SS-Obersturmführer* Brausewetter
(*Stabsscharführer*)	*SS-Hauptscharführer* Busse

	1. Kompanie
2/2/45-2/15/45	*SS-Obersturmführer* Atz
2/20/45- 5/45	*SS-Obersturmführer* Steiner
(*Stabsscharführer*)	*SS-Hauptscharführer* Fischer
2. Kompanie	
	***SS-Obersturmführer* Stauch**
Entire Battalion	Military Postal Service Number 20 686

SS-Panzerjäger-Abteilung 32

Kommandeur	SS-Sturmbannführer Neuenfeld
Abteilungsarzt	*SS-Untersturmführer* Strauß
Chief 1. Kompanie	*SS-Obersturmführer* Schöttle
3. Kompanie	*SS-Untersturmführer* Stachon
4. Kompanie	*SS-Hauptsturmführer* Krauß
Entire Detachment	Military Postal Service Number 37 196

SS-Flak-Abteilung 32

Kommandeur	*SS-Hauptsturmführer* Löschnigg
Adjutant	*SS-Untersturmführer* Schwarz
Stabsscharführer	*SS-Hauptscharführer* Ermisch
Chief 1. Batterie	*SS-Obersturmführer* Hübner
Chief 2. Batterie	*SS-Obersturmführer* Deuschle
Chief 3. Batterie	*SS-Obersturmführer* Hiebler
Staff	*Military Postal Service Number 31 765*
1. Batterie	*Military Postal Service Number 64 273*
2. Batterie	*Military Postal Service Number 66 779*
3. Batterie	*Military Postal Service Number 67 964*

SS-Nachrichten-Abteilung 32

Abteilungskommandeur *SS-Sturmbannführer* Barton
Funkkompanie *SS-Obersturmführer* Fauland
Military Postal Service Number 21 641

SS-Feldersatz-Bataillon 32

1. Kompanie *SS-Untersturmführer* Deuschle
Military Postal Service Number 05 066

SS-Füsilier-Bataillon 32

Bataillonskommandeur SS-*Hauptsturmführer Kling*
Military Postal Service Number 36 652

SS-Versorgungsregiment 32

Staff *Military Postal Service Number 38 280*
Bäckerei/Schlachterei *Military Postal Service Number 22 608*
Remainder *Military Postal Service Number 37 569*

SS-Wirtschaftsbataillon 32

Military Postal Service Number 38 280

SS-Sanitäts-Kompanie 32

Military Postal Service Number 39 339

SS-Veterinär-Kompanie 32

Military Postal Service Number 23 045

SS-Feldpostamt 32

Military Postal Service Number 27 186

11

Footnote Index

12/15/23 Adam, Günter: Die 32. SS-Panzer-Grenadier-Division "30. Januar" an der Oder, in: *Der Freiwillige*, Osnabrück

5/6/7/8/87, sowie verschiedene Korrespondenz 1992/93

6/14/19/20/21/22 Baumgart, Eberhard: Halbe-Halbe in: *Der Freiwillige*, Osnabrück

2/3/4/5/6/90, sowie verschiedene Korrespondenz 1992/93 und Archiv Baumgart

24 Darges, Fritz: Hans Kempin in: *Der Freiwillige*, Osnabrück 2/93, S. 28

1/11 Haupt, Werner: *Das Ende im Osten*, Dorheim 1970

9/10 Förster, Gerhard, Lakowski, Richard: 1945 – Das Jahr der endgültigen Niederlage der faschistischen Wehrmacht – Dokumente, Berlin 1985[2]

2 Hausser, Paul: *Soldaten wie andere auch*, Osnabrück 1988[3]

2 Klietmann, K.G.: *Die Waffen-SS – Eine Dokumentation*, Osnabrück 1965

24 Krätschmer, Ernst-Günther: *Die Ritterkreuzträger der Waffen-SS*, Preußisch-Oldendorf 1982[3], S. 329, 637, 881

2/7/11 Leuthen, Hans: 32. SS-Freiwilligen-Grenadier-Division "30. Januar" in: *Der Freiwillige*, Osnabrück 5/6/90

4/7/18 Polle, Jochen, Wilke, Horst: Pioniereinheiten der 32. SS-Freiwilligen-Grenadier-Division "30. Januar," o.O.a. 1987, sowie verschiedene Korrespondenz 1992/93

5 Stöber, Hans: *Die Flugabwehrverbände der Waffen-SS*, 1984

3 Tieke, Wilhelm: *Aufstellung, Einsatz und Untergang der SS-Panzerbrigade "Westfalen,"* Gummersbach 1990

7/11/13/16 Tieke, Wilhelm: *Das Ende zwischen Oder und Elbe*, Stuttgart 1992^2

8 Vahldiek, Walter: *Die Werfer-Abteilungen der ehemaligen Waffen-SS*, Düsseldorf 1958, sowie verschiedene Korrespondenz 1992

17 ohne, *Die Wehrmachtsbericht 1939-1945*, Band III, München, 1985

12

Documents

The documents here provide a glimpse into the events of the *32. SS-Division "30. Januar"* at the time. They include the regrouping from a motorized to horse-drawn division through horse registers, show transfers, tickets, sympathy letters to fallen soldiers' bereaved, etc. No explanation is necessary, the documents speak for themselves.

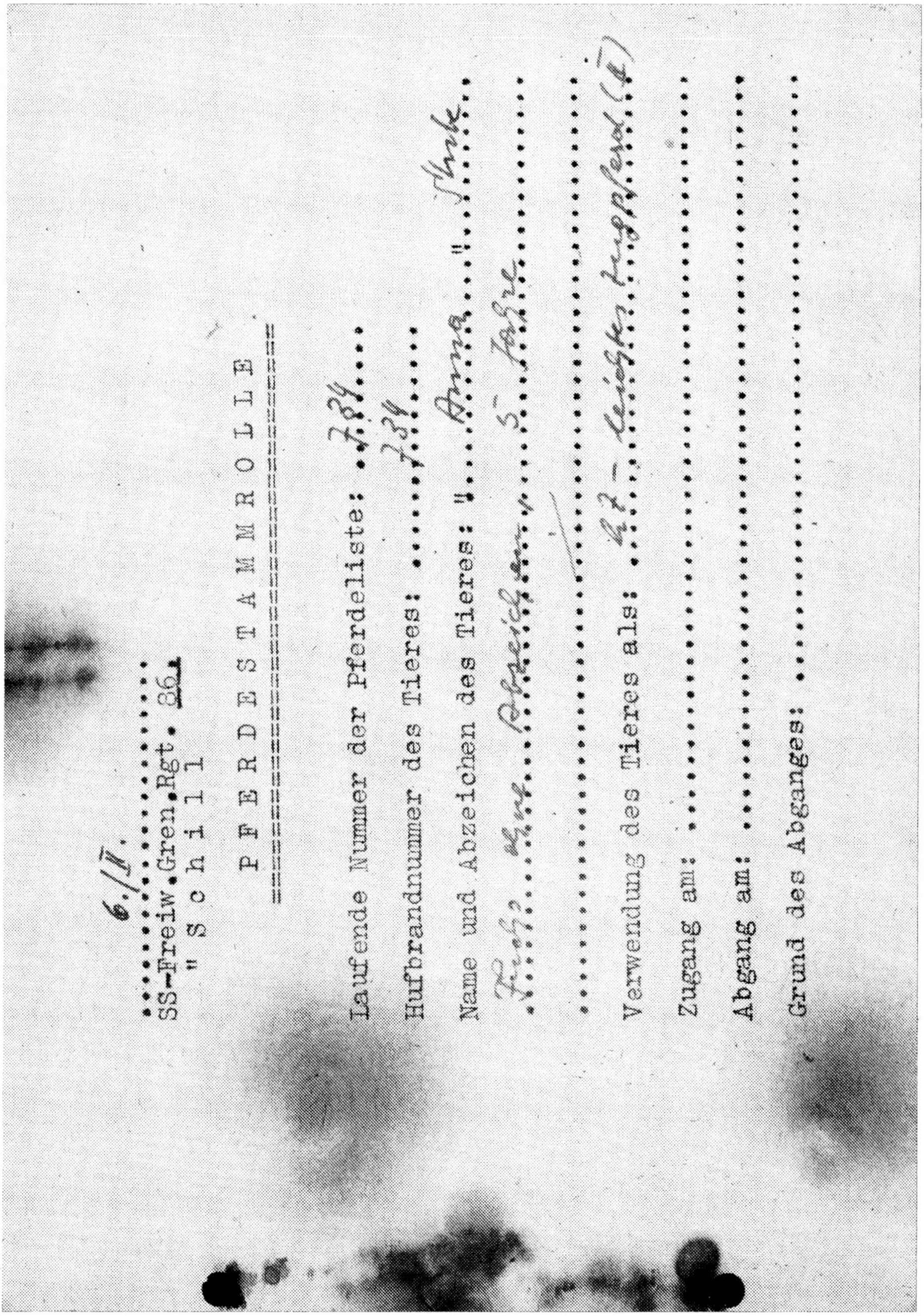

6./II.

SS-Freiw.Gren.Rgt. 86.
"S c h i l l"

P F E R D E S T A M M R O L L E

Laufende Nummer der Pferdeliste: 784

Hufbrandnummer des Tieres: 784

Name und Abzeichen des Tieres: "Anna" Stute

Fuchs, ohne Abzeichen, 5 Jahre

Verwendung des Tieres als: lt. - leichtes Zugpferd (lt)

Zugang am:

Abgang am:

Grund des Abganges:

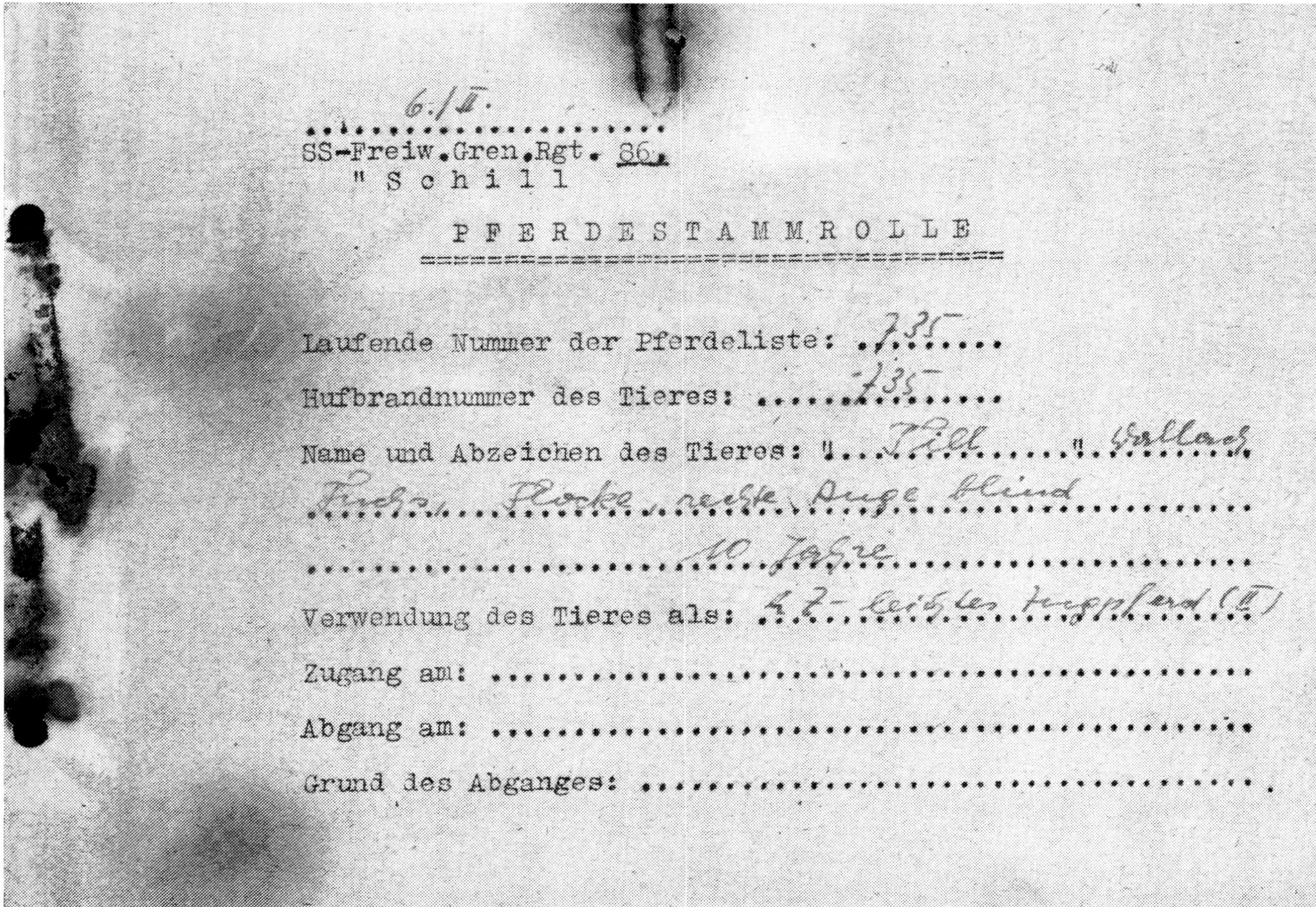

6./III.

SS-Freiw.Gren.Rgt. 86.
"Schill

P F E R D E S T A M M R O L L E

Laufende Nummer der Pferdeliste: 735

Hufbrandnummer des Tieres: 735

Name und Abzeichen des Tieres: "Till" Wallach
Fuchs, Blesse, rechte Auge blind
10 Jahre

Verwendung des Tieres als: L.Z.-leichtes Zugpferd (III)

Zugang am:

Abgang am:

Grund des Abganges:

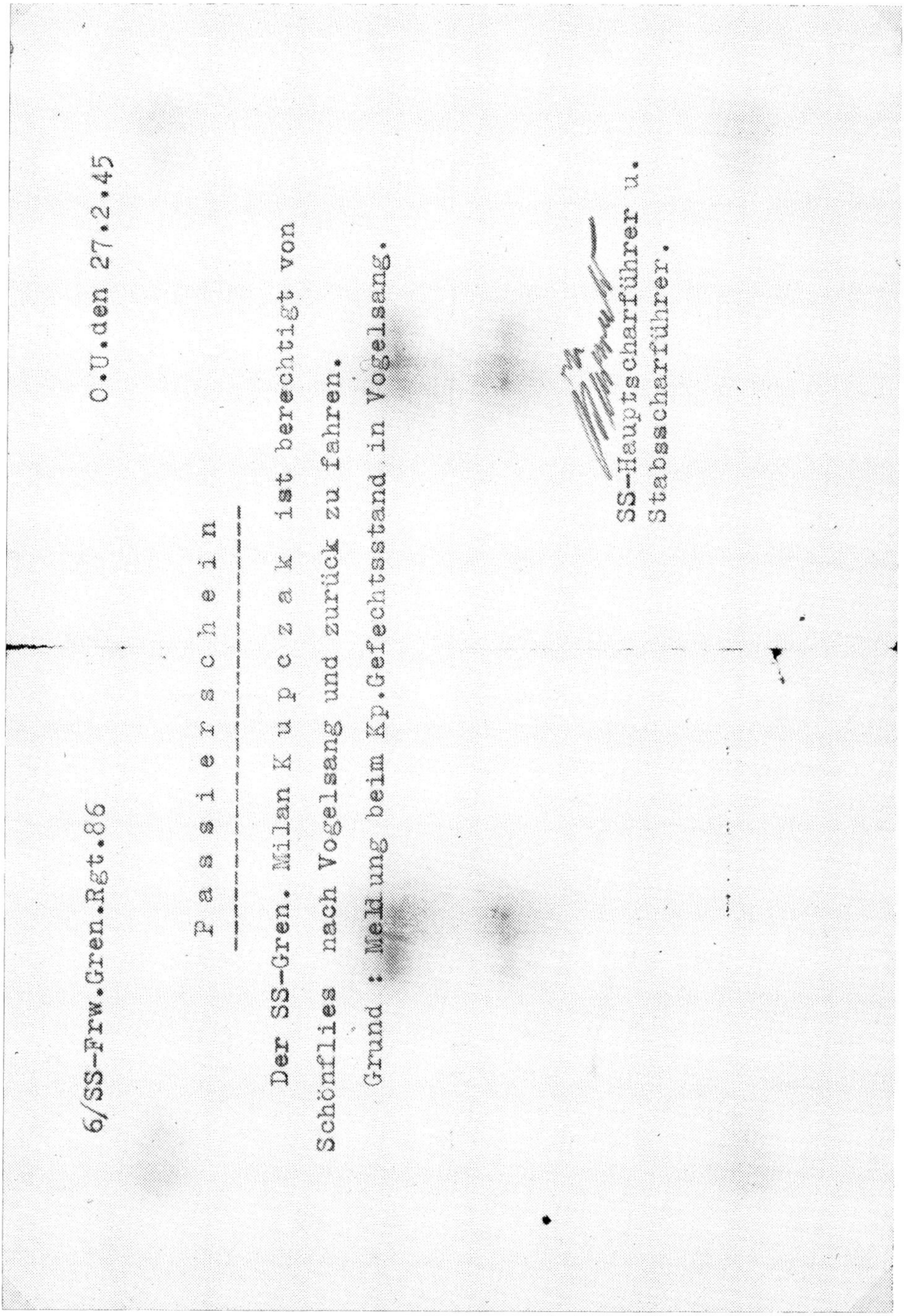

6/SS-Frw.Gren.Rgt.86 O.U.den 27.2.45

P a s s i e r s c h e i n

Der SS-Gren. Milan K u p c z a k ist berechtigt von Schönflies nach Vogelsang und zurück zu fahren.

Grund : Meldung beim Kp.Gefechtsstand in Vogelsang.

SS-Hauptscharführer u.
Stabsscharführer.

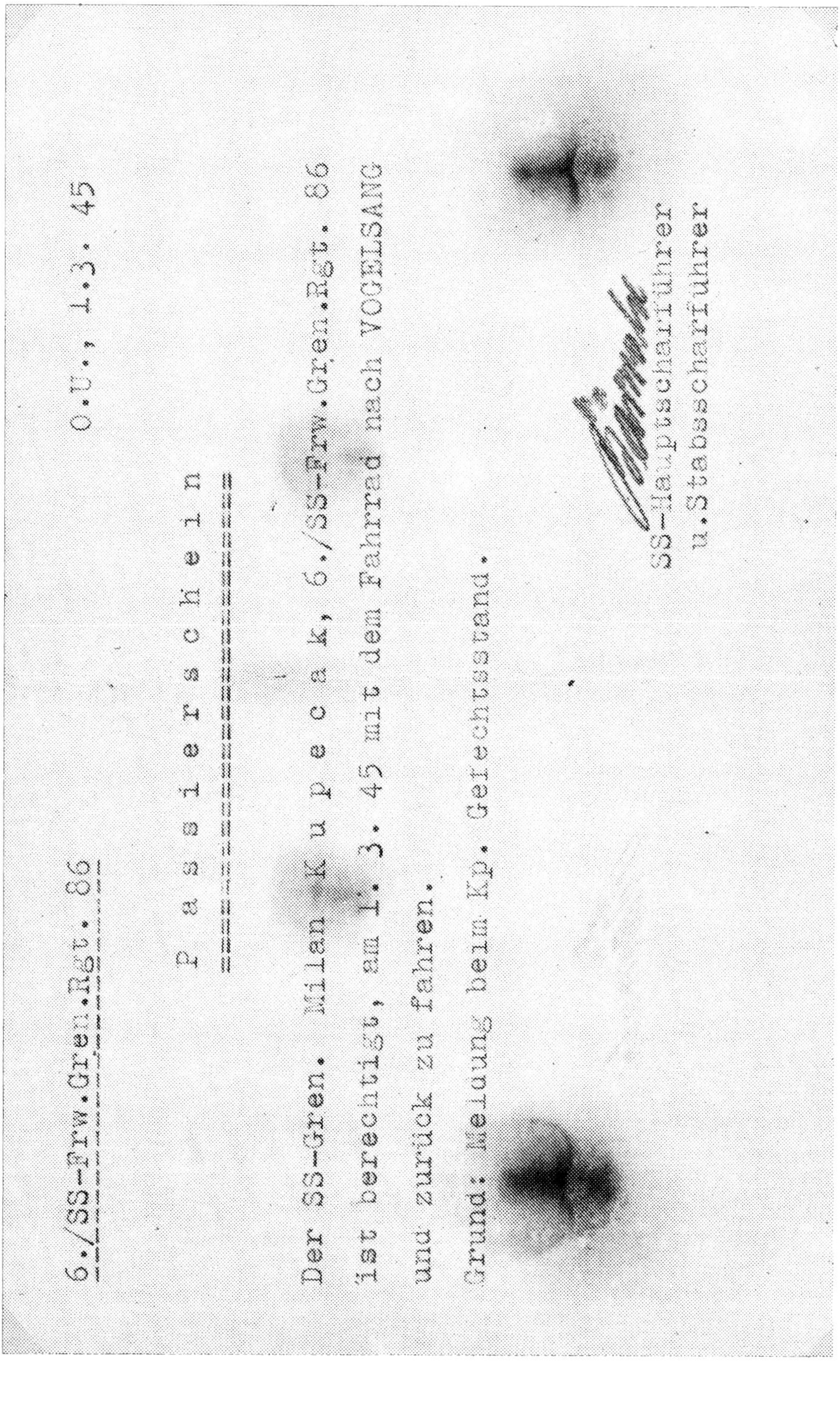
6./SS-Frw.Gren.Rgt. 86 O.U., 1.3. 45

P a s s i e r s c h e i n

Der SS-Gren. Milan K u p e c a k, 6./SS-Frw.Gren.Rgt. 86
ist berechtigt, am 1. 3. 45 mit dem Fahrrad nach VOGELSANG
und zurück zu fahren.

Grund: Meldung beim Kp. Gerechtsstand.

SS-Hauptscharführer
u.Stabsscharführer

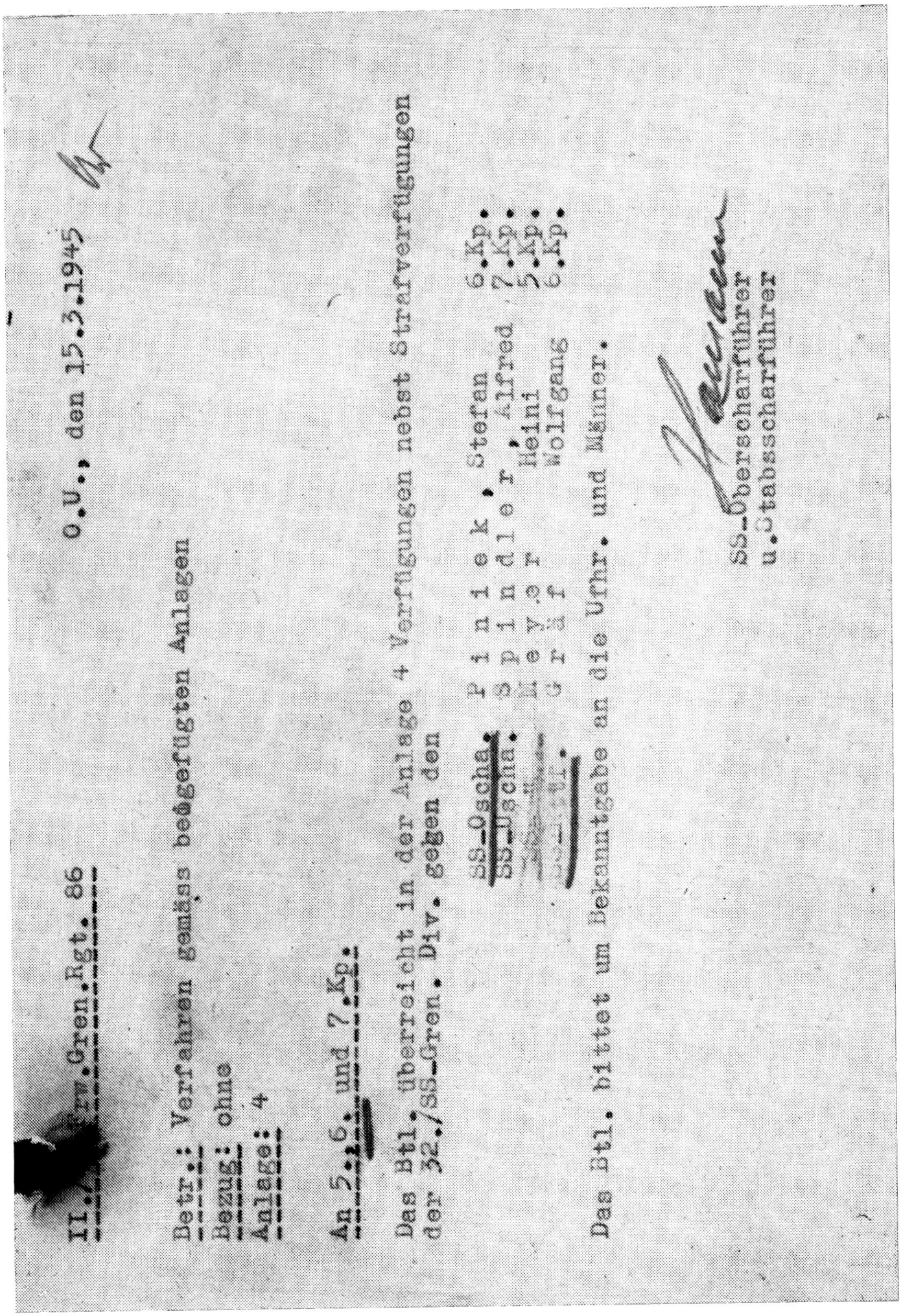

II./ ... Frw.Gren.Rgt. 86 O.U., den 15.3.1945

Betr.: Verfahren gemäss beigefügten Anlagen
Bezug: ohne
Anlage: 4

An 5., 6. und 7.Kp.

Das Btl. überreicht in der Anlage 4 Verfügungen nebst Strafverfügungen der 32./SS-Gren. Div. gegen den

SS-Oscha. P i n i e k , Stefan 6.Kp.
SS-Uscha. S p i n d l e r , Alfred 7.Kp.
[illegible] M e y e r Heini 5.Kp.
[illegible] G r ä f Wolfgang 6.Kp.

Das Btl. bittet um Bekanntgabe an die Uffhr. und Männer.

SS-Oberscharführer
u.Stabsscharführer

Feldgericht der
32. SS-Frw.Gren.Div."3o.Januar"

(Gericht)

10.3.45

O.U., den 9. März 1945

St. L. ______ Nr. 44 /1945

U.R.

an Feldersatz-Btl.32
Gerichts-SS-Führer

1 Anlage.

mit dem Ersuchen, de[m] Beschuldigten die anliegende Strafverfügung mündlich zu verkünden und auszuhändigen — durch einen SS-Führer, ~~Polizei-Offizier oder Beamten~~ mündlich verkünden und aushändigen zu lassen.

Der Beschuldigte kann bis zum Ablauf des dritten Tages, der auf den Tag der Bekanntgabe folgt, schriftlich oder mündlich Einspruch gegen die Strafverfügung erheben oder auf den Einspruch verzichten. Diese Erklärungen können auch Sie oder der von Ihnen mit der Bekanntgabe der Strafverfügung beauftragte SS-Führer, ~~Polizei-Offizier oder Beamte~~ entgegennehmen. Ein etwaiger Verzicht auf den Einspruch ist unverzüglich zu melden. Sonst ist spätestens am 4. Tage, der auf den Tag der Bekanntgabe der Strafverfügung folgt, zu melden, ob Einspruch erhoben ist oder nicht. Der Einspruch kann innerhalb der Einspruchsfrist ohne weiteres, nach diesem Zeitpunkt bis zur Verkündung des Urteils nur mit Zustimmung des Gerichtsherrn oder des Gerichts zurückgenommen werden.

Für die Meldung ist das umseitige Formblatt zu benutzen. Nichtzutreffendes ist darin zu streichen. ~~Kann dem Beschuldigten die Zahlung der Geldstrafe in einer Summe nach Ihrem Ermessen nicht zugemutet werden, so ist dies anzugeben.~~

Die Vollstreckung der Strafe ist erst auf besondere Anordnung durchzuführen.

SS-Untersturmführer und
Gerich~~ts-SS-Führer~~

_______________ , den _______________ 194__

Meldung

An den Gerichtsherrn

über Feldgericht der 32.SS.Frw.Gren.Div.
(Gericht)

Dem SS-Rottenführer Karl, Otto, Wolfgang Gräf,

habe ich die Strafverfügung vom 8. März 1945

St.L. ______ Nr. 45/1945 am ______

mündlich verkündet und ausgehändigt.

Erster Fall: Der Beschuldigte erhebt Einspruch.

Der Beschuldigte hat am ______ mündlich — durch beiliegendes Schriftstück — bei mir Einspruch erhoben und zur Begründung angeführt:

______

______

______

______

Zusatz bei verspätetem Einspruch:
Der Beschuldigte war an der Abgabe einer fristgemäßen Erklärung nicht verhindert — dadurch verhindert, daß er ______

______

Zweiter Fall: Der Beschuldigte gibt keine Erklärung ab.

Der Beschuldigte hat mir bis zum Ablauf des ______

______ (des dritten Tages, der auf den Tag der Bekanntgabe folgt) keine Erklärung über den Einspruch abgegeben, obwohl er dazu in der Lage gewesen wäre.

Dritter Fall: Der Beschuldigte verzichtet auf Einspruch.

Der Beschuldigte hat mir am ______ erklärt, daß er auf Einspruch verzichte.

______
(Unterschrift mit Dienstgrad und Dienststellung)

Bestell-Nr.: W# - 5935 Meldung
#-Vordruckverlag W. F. Mayr, Miesbach (Bayer. Hochland) 20081

Beglaubigte Abschrift.

Feldgericht der Dienststelle
Feldpostnummer 05 662

(Gericht)

Div.Gef.Std. den 8. März 1945

St.L. Nr. 45/1945

An
SS-Rottenführer
Karl, Otto Wolfgang G r ä f,
8./SS-Pz.Gren.A.u.E.Btl.1 jetzt:Feldersatz-Btl. 32

geboren am 3. 9. 1923 in [illegible]

Strafverfügung

Sie werden beschuldigt, sich am 26.2.1945

in Spreenhagen
einer gemeinschaftlichen unvorsichtigen Behandlung von Waffen und Munition,
schuldig gemacht zu haben, indem Sie gemeinsam mit dem SS-Unterscharführer M e y e r den Plan fassten, den in gehobener Stimmung befindlichen Stabsscharführer, SS-Oberscharführer P i n i e k zu verulken und einen widerrechtlich zurückgehaltenen Kanonenschlag holten, der nach Kürzung der Zündschnur dem Stabsscharführer P i n i e k vor die Tür gelegt wurde, um ihn und seine Gäste durch den Knall zu erschrecken.
Der SS-Hauptscharführer L a n g e r hörte etwas von den Vorbereitungen an der Türe, lief hinaus und nahm den Kanonenschlag in die Hand. Dieser detonierte ihm vor der Brust und verletzte ihn tötlich.

— Vergehen — strafbar nach § 148 MStGB, §47 RStGB.

Bestell-Nr.: WH [illegible] Strafverfügung.
W-Vordruckverlag W. [illegible], Miesbach (Bayer. Hochland) [illegible]

Beweismittel sind: **Geständnis**

Es wird deshalb gegen Sie eine Strafe von

3 -drei- Monaten Gefängnis

(in Buchstaben:

) ~~Reichsmark~~

— ~~Gefängnis — Haft —~~ ~~Arrest~~ festgesetzt.

~~Wird die Geldstrafe nicht bezahlt, so tritt an Stelle von je~~

(in Buchstaben:) Reichsmark

eine Freiheitsstrafe von (in Buchstaben:

Tagen Haft — Gefängnis.—

Diese Strafverfügung wird vollstreckbar, wenn Sie nicht bis zum Ablauf des 3. Tages, der auf den Tag der Bekanntgabe folgt, Einspruch erheben. Den Einspruch können Sie schriftlich oder mündlich beim Gericht (Gerichtsherrn), Ihrem nächsten Disziplinarvorgesetzten, oder bei demjenigen, der Ihnen die Strafverfügung bekanntgegeben hat, erheben.

Sie können vor Ablauf der drei Tage auf den Einspruch verzichten.

~~Die Geldstrafe ist binnen einer Woche nach Eintritt der Vollstreckbarkeit an~~

Nach Eintritt der Rechtskraft ist ein Teil der Strafe in Höhe von 2-zwei-Wochen als gesch. Arrest im Strafvollstreckungszug zu vollstrecken; der Rest wird zwecks Bewährung bei der eigenen Einheit ausgesetzt.
Bei Einspruch kann gegen Sie ev. eine höhere Strafe verhängt werden.

~~zu zahlen.~~ Sie kann in monatlichen Teilbeträgen von Reichsmark, zahlbar spätestens am jeden Monats, erstmalig am entrichtet werden.

Geht die Strafe nicht pünktlich ein, so wird die Zwangsvollstreckung oder die Vollstreckung der Ersatzfreiheitsstrafe veranlaßt.

Der Gerichtsherr:	Der Untersuchungsführer:
gez. A x	gez. Dr. P a t i g.
SS-Oberführer und Div.Kommandeur	SS-Hauptsturmführer und SS-Richter d.R.

f.d.R.d.A.

[signature]

SS-Hauptscharführer

Feldgericht der
32.SS-Frw.Gren.Div."3o. Januar"
(Gericht)

10.3.45

O.U., den 9. März 1945

St. L. Nr. 45 /1945

U.R.

an Feldersatz-Btl.32
~~Gerichts-SS-Führer~~

1 Anlage.

mit dem Ersuchen, dem Beschuldigten die anliegende Strafverfügung mündlich zu verkünden und auszuhändigen — durch einen SS-Führer, ~~Polizei-Offizier oder Beamten~~ mündlich verkünden und aushändigen zu lassen.

Der Beschuldigte kann bis zum Ablauf des dritten Tages, der auf den Tag der Bekanntgabe folgt, schriftlich oder mündlich Einspruch gegen die Strafverfügung erheben oder auf den Einspruch verzichten. Diese Erklärungen können auch Sie oder der von Ihnen mit der Bekanntgabe der Strafverfügung beauftragte SS-Führer, ~~Polizei-Offizier oder Beamte~~ entgegennehmen. Ein etwaiger Verzicht auf den Einspruch ist unverzüglich zu melden. Sonst ist spätestens am 4. Tage, der auf den Tag der Bekanntgabe der Strafverfügung folgt, zu melden, ob Einspruch erhoben ist oder nicht. Der Einspruch kann innerhalb der Einspruchsfrist ohne weiteres, nach diesem Zeitpunkt bis zur Verkündung des Urteils nur mit Zustimmung des Gerichtsherrn oder des Gerichts zurückgenommen werden.

Für die Meldung ist das umseitige Formblatt zu benutzen. Nichtzutreffendes ist darin zu streichen. ~~Kann dem Beschuldigten die Zahlung der Geldstrafe in einer Summe nach Ihrem Ermessen nicht zugemutet werden, so ist dies anzugeben.~~

Die Vollstreckung der Strafe ist erst auf besondere Anordnung durchzuführen.

SS-Untersturmführer und
Gerichts-SS-Führer
(Dienstgrad und Dienststellung)

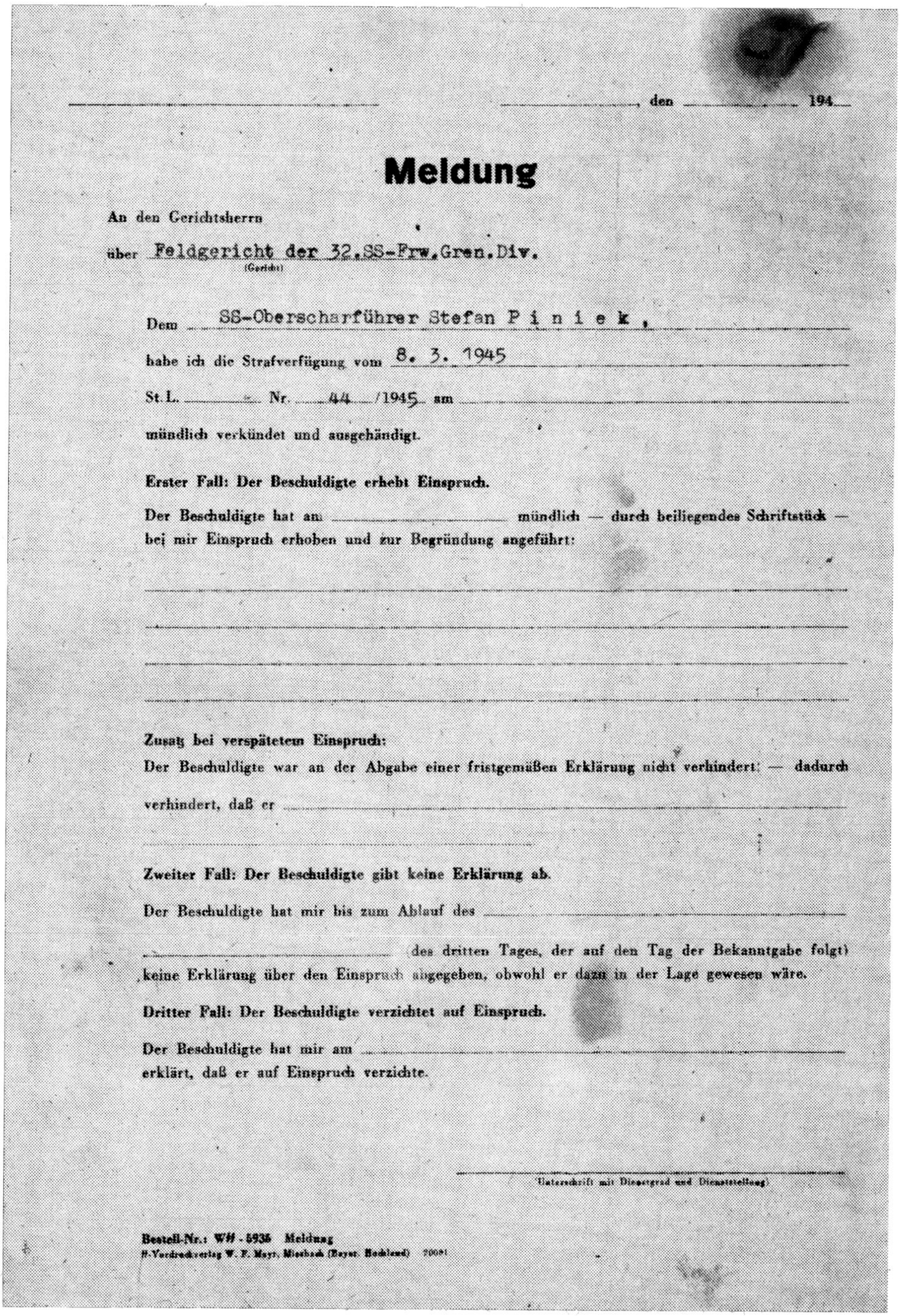

__________ den ________ 194_

Meldung

An den Gerichtsherrn

über Feldgericht der 32.SS-Frw.Gren.Div.
(Gericht)

Dem SS-Oberscharführer Stefan P i n i e k,

habe ich die Strafverfügung vom 8. 3. 1945

St.L. ____ Nr. 44 /1945 am ________

mündlich verkündet und ausgehändigt.

Erster Fall: Der Beschuldigte erhebt Einspruch.

Der Beschuldigte hat am ________ mündlich — durch beiliegendes Schriftstück — bei mir Einspruch erhoben und zur Begründung angeführt:

Zusatz bei verspätetem Einspruch:

Der Beschuldigte war an der Abgabe einer fristgemäßen Erklärung nicht verhindert. — dadurch verhindert, daß er ________

Zweiter Fall: Der Beschuldigte gibt keine Erklärung ab.

Der Beschuldigte hat mir bis zum Ablauf des ________ (des dritten Tages, der auf den Tag der Bekanntgabe folgt) keine Erklärung über den Einspruch abgegeben, obwohl er dazu in der Lage gewesen wäre.

Dritter Fall: Der Beschuldigte verzichtet auf Einspruch.

Der Beschuldigte hat mir am ________ erklärt, daß er auf Einspruch verzichte.

____
(Unterschrift mit Dienstgrad und Dienststellung)

Bestell-Nr.: W# - 5935 Meldung
#-Vordruckverlag W. F. Mayr, Miesbach (Bayer. Hochland) 20081

Beglaubigte Abschrift.

Feldgericht der Dienststelle
Feldpostnummer 05 662
(Gericht)

Div.Gef.Std., den 8. März 1945

StL. Nr. 44 /1945

An

SS-Oberscharführer Stefan P i n i e k,

8./SS-Pz.Gren.A.u.E.Btl.1 jetzt Feldersatz-Btl.32

geboren am 31.8. 1917 in [illegible]

Strafverfügung

Sie werden beschuldigt, sich am 26.2.1945

in Spreenhagen

eines rechtswidrigen Waffengebrauches
schuldig gemacht zu haben, indem Sie nach Genuss von etwa
1o - 12 Glas Schnapses in gehobener Stimmung mit der Pistole
im Zimmer herumschossen. Sie schossen, ohne bestimmte Ziele,
in den Kohlenkasten und gegen die Zimmerwand.

— ~~Übertretung~~ — Vergehen — ~~Verbrechen~~ strafbar nach § 149 MStGB.

Bestell-Nr.: WH - 5934 Strafverfügung.
H-Vordruckverlag W. F. Mayr, Miesbach (Bayer. Hochland) 20085

Beweismittel sind: **Geständnis**

Es wird deshalb gegen Sie eine Strafe von

2 -zwei- Monaten Gefängnis

(~~in Buchstaben~~:

) ~~Reichsmark~~

— ~~Gefängnis — Haft —~~ ~~Arrest~~ festgesetzt.

~~Wird die Geldstrafe nicht bezahlt, so tritt an Stelle von je~~

(in Buchstaben:) Reichsmark

eine Freiheitsstrafe von (in Buchstaben:

~~Tagen Haft — Gefängnis.~~ –

Diese Strafverfügung wird vollstreckbar, wenn Sie nicht bis zum Ablauf des 3. Tages, der auf den Tag der Bekanntgabe folgt, Einspruch erheben. Den Einspruch können Sie schriftlich oder mündlich beim Gericht (Gerichtsherrn), Ihrem nächsten Disziplinarvorgesetzten, oder bei demjenigen, der Ihnen die Strafverfügung bekanntgegeben hat, erheben. Sie können vor Ablauf der drei Tage auf den Einspruch verzichten.

~~Die Geldstrafe ist binnen einer Woche nach Eintritt der Vollstreckbarkeit an~~

Nach Eintritt der Rechtskraft ist ein Teil der Strafe in Höhe von einer Woche in Form des gelinden Arrestes im Strafvollstreckungszug zu vollstrecken; der Rest wird zwecks Bewährung bei der eigenen Einheit ausgesetzt.
Im Falle des Einspruches kann gegen Sie ev.eine höhere Strafe verhängt werde n.

~~zu zahlen. Sie kann in monatlichen Teilbeträgen von Reichsmark, zahlbar~~

~~spätestens am jeden Monats, erstmalig am entrichtet werden.~~

~~Geht die Strafe nicht pünktlich ein, so wird die Zwangsvollstreckung oder die Vollstreckung der Ersatzfreiheitsstrafe veranlaßt.~~

Der Gerichtsherr:	Der Untersuchungsführer:
gez. A x	gez. Dr. P a t i g
SS-Oberführer und Divisionskommandeur	SS-Hauptsturmführer und SS-Richter d. R.

f.d.R.d.A.
Leisner.
SS-Hauptscharführer

Stefan Piniek was born on 31 August 1917, in Groß-Leschetz. Already in the *Leibstandarte-SS* Adolf Hitler before the outbreak of war, in spring 1945 he was *SS-Oberscharführer* in the *8./SS-Pz-Gren-Ausb.* and *Ersatzbtl 1* in Spreenhagen. At the beginning of March 1945 he was transferred to the *SS-Feldersatzbataillon 32*. He was already released from Soviet war captivity on 23 December 1945.

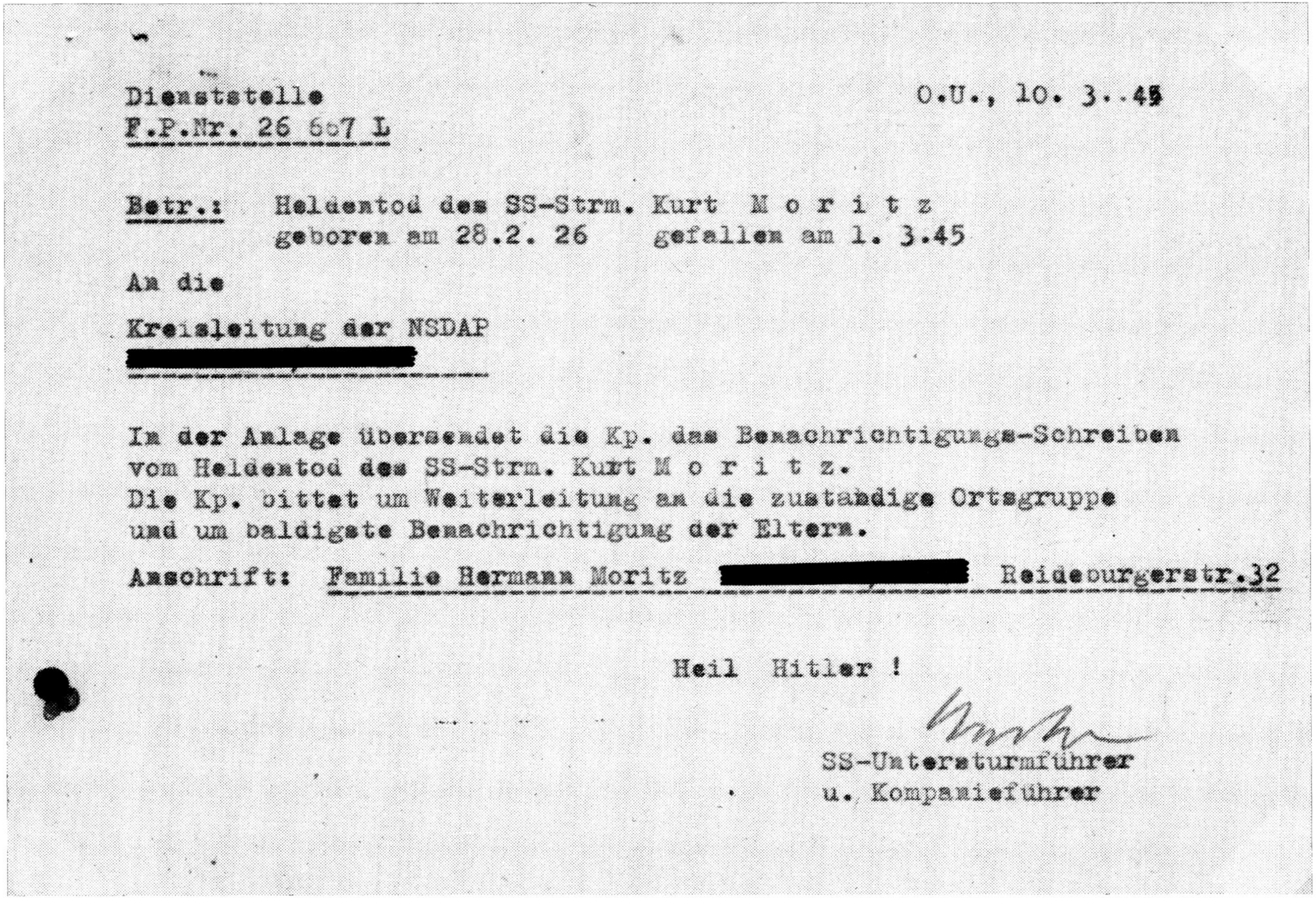

Dienststelle
F.P.Nr. 26 607 L

O.U., 10. 3..45

Betr.: Heldentod des SS-Strm. Kurt M o r i t z
geboren am 28.2. 26 gefallen am 1. 3.45

An die

Kreisleitung der NSDAP

Im der Anlage übersendet die Kp. das Benachrichtigungs-Schreiben
vom Heldentod des SS-Strm. Kurt M o r i t z.
Die Kp. bittet um Weiterleitung an die zustandige Ortsgruppe
und um baldigste Benachrichtigung der Eltern.

Anschrift: Familie Hermann Moritz Reideburgerstr.32

Heil Hitler !

SS-Untersturmführer
u. Kompanieführer

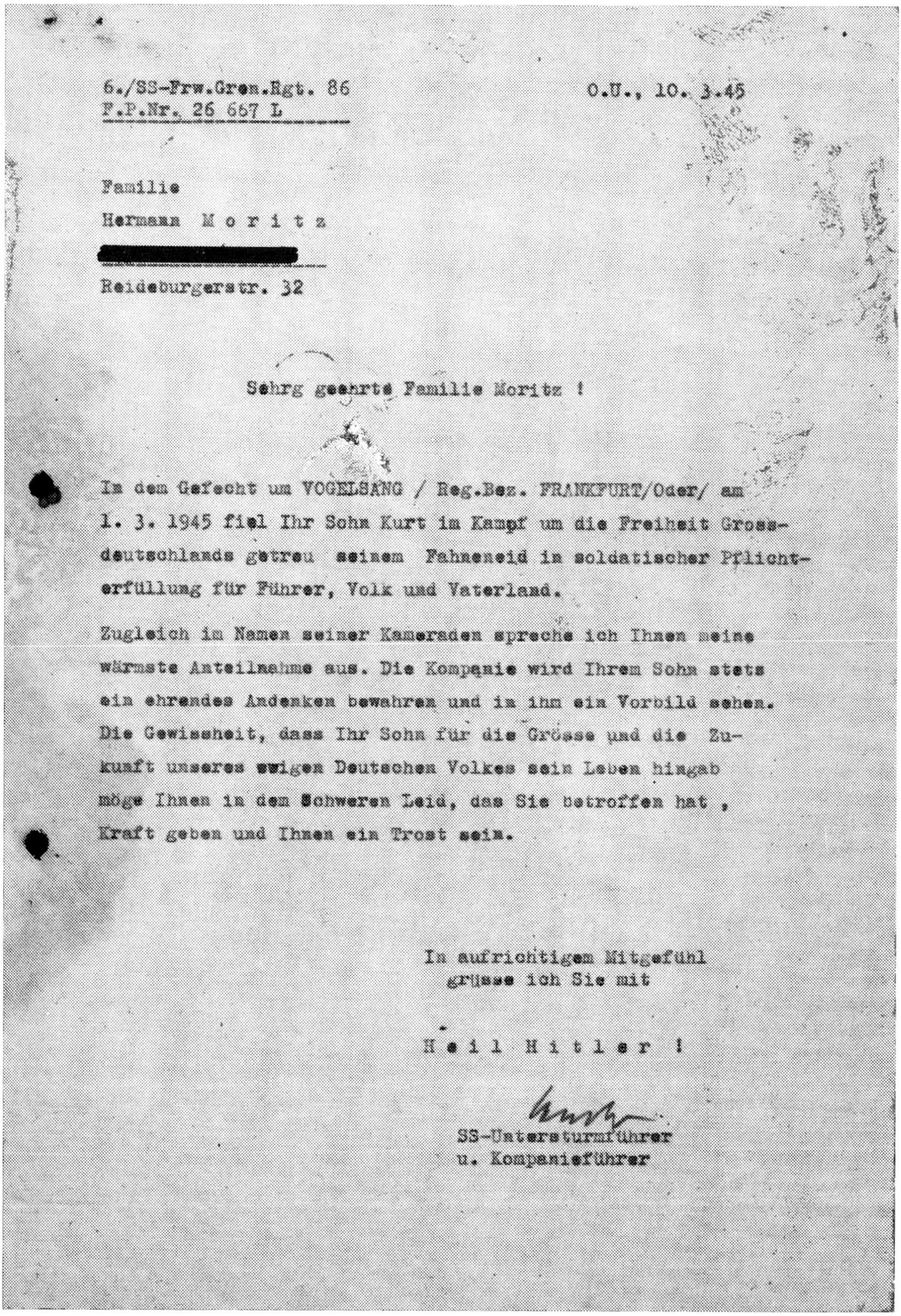

6./SS-Frw.Gren.Rgt. 86
F.P.Nr. 26 667 L

O.U., 10. 3.45

Familie

Hermann M o r i t z

Reideburgerstr. 32

Sehrg geehrte Familie Moritz !

In dem Gefecht um VOGELSANG / Reg.Bez. FRANKFURT/Oder/ am 1. 3. 1945 fiel Ihr Sohn Kurt im Kampf um die Freiheit Grossdeutschlands getreu seinem Fahneneid in soldatischer Pflichterfüllung für Führer, Volk und Vaterland.

Zugleich im Namen seiner Kameraden spreche ich Ihnen meine wärmste Anteilnahme aus. Die Kompanie wird Ihrem Sohn stets ein ehrendes Andenken bewahren und in ihm ein Vorbild sehen. Die Gewissheit, dass Ihr Sohn für die Grösse und die Zukunft unseres ewigen Deutschen Volkes sein Leben hingab möge Ihnen in dem Schweren Leid, das Sie betroffen hat , Kraft geben und Ihnen ein Trost sein.

In aufrichtigem Mitgefühl
grüsse ich Sie mit

H e i l H i t l e r !

SS-Untersturmführer
u. Kompanieführer

U ./SS-Frw.Gren.Rgt. 86 Lfd. Nr. ~~129~~ 140
(Komp., Batl., Regt., Div.)

Namentliche Verlustmeldung

an

SS-F. H. A. / Amt V, IIb

(dreifach)

1	Familienname	M o r i t z
2	Vorname	Kurt
3	Geburtstag, -ort, -kreis	28. 2. 26 [blacked out]
4	Dienstgrad	SS-Sturmmann
5	Erkennungsmarke	III./SS-Pz.Gren.Ausb. Rgt. -295-
6	Familienstand	ledig
7	Ort, Tag und Zeitpunkt des Verl.	1.3. 45 Vogelsang
8	Gefallen[1])	Gra. Spl. Kopf
9	Verwundet[1]) schwer	---
	Verwundet[1]) leicht	---
9a	Körperstelle u. Waffe[2])	---
10	Gefangen	---
11	Vermißt oder sonst.	---
12	Gestorben außerhalb der Lazarettbehandlung an Verwundung	---
12a	Gestorben außerhalb der Lazarettbehandlung an Krankheit	---
12b	Gestorben außerhalb der Lazarettbehandlung an Unfall	---
12c	Gestorben außerhalb der Lazarettbehandlung an Selbstmord	---
12d	Gestorben außerhalb der Lazarettbehandlung an Vollstrecktes Todesurteil	---
13	Verbleib des Toten, Verwundeten oder Verletzten An welche Sanitätsdienststelle abgegeben	Beigesetzt Heldenfriedhof Fünfeichen Feld 2 Reihe 5 Nr. 24 v.links
14	Genaue Grablage	"
15	Letzter Wohnsitz (falls Berufssoldat, Heimatstandort des Friedenstruppenteils)	[blacked out] Reideburgerstr. 32
16	Anschrift der nächsten Angehörigen unter Angabe des Verwandtschaftsverhältnisses	Vater: Hermann Moritz wie 15

Bestell-Nr. W SS 4393

Metten & Co. Berlin SW 61

17	Angehörige benachrichtigt	am 10. 3. 45
18	Staatsangehörigkeit	D.R.
19	Volkszugehörigkeit	—
20	Einberufen durch ᛋᛋ-Erg.-Stelle	SS-Erg.St..Elbe IV
21	Eintritt in die Waffen-ᛋᛋ	25. 3. 1944
22		
23		
24		

SS-Ustuf. u. Kp.Fhr.

Raum für Skizze und Kampfbericht bei Vermißten oder Gefangenen

Grablage:

Heldenfriedhof Fünfeichen / Oder

Feld 2
Reihe 5
Nr.: 24

[1] **Abkürzungen:** K. = Kopf, H. = Hals, Br. = Brust, Ba. = Bauch, R. = Rücken, l. A. = linker Arm, (I.G. = Inf.-Gesch., H.Gr. = Handgranaten-Verl., Gs.V. = Kampfstoffvergiftung, A.G = Art.Gesch.).

[2] Hierzu rechnen auch Verstauchung und Verrenkung durch stumpfe Gewalt infolge feindlicher Einwirkung durch Verschüttung usw.

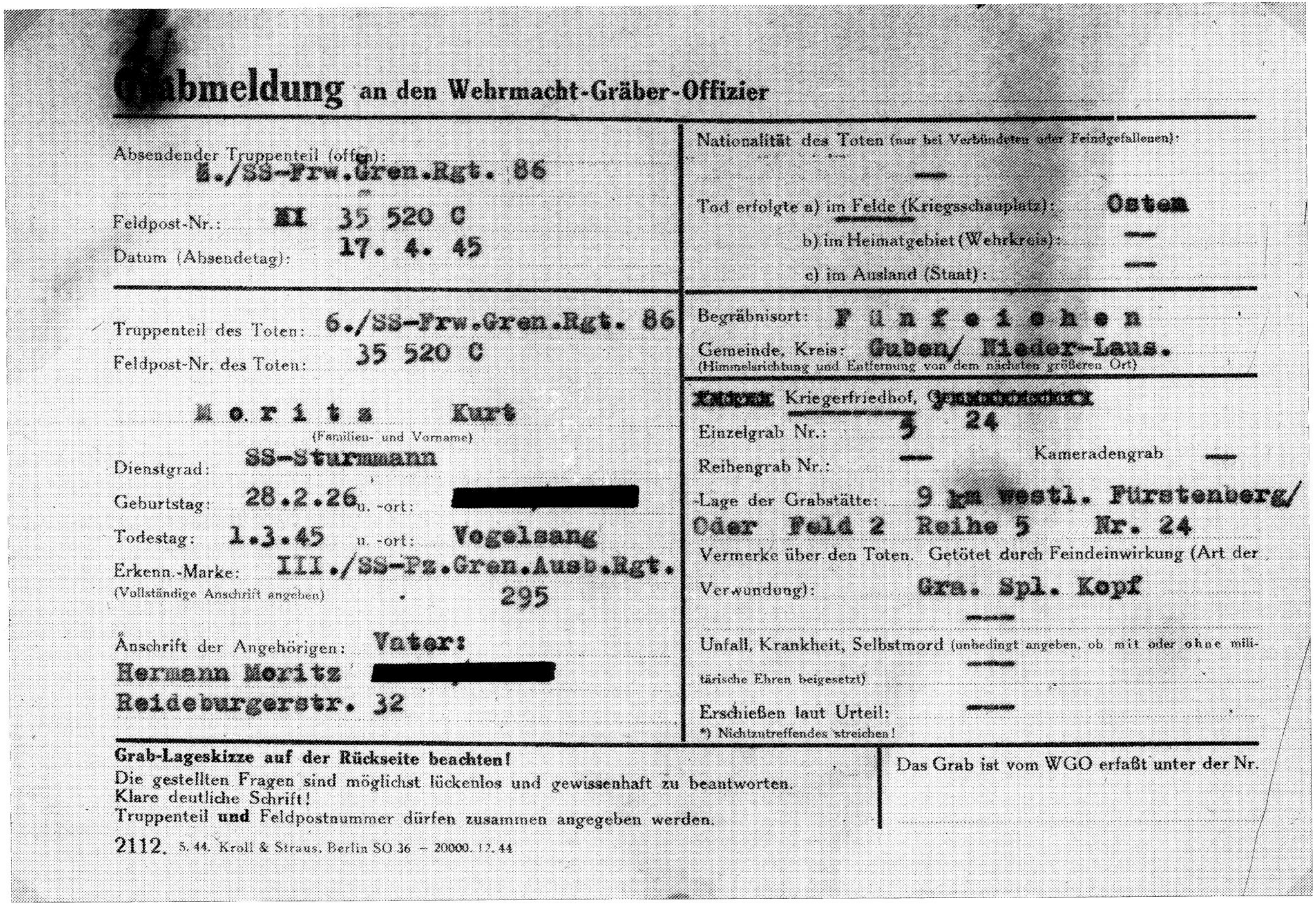

Grabmeldung an den Wehrmacht-Gräber-Offizier

Absendender Truppenteil (offen): 6./SS-Frw.Gren.Rgt. 86

Feldpost-Nr.: XI 35 520 C

Datum (Absendetag): 17. 4. 45

Truppenteil des Toten: 6./SS-Frw.Gren.Rgt. 86

Feldpost-Nr. des Toten: 35 520 C

Moritz Kurt
(Familien- und Vorname)

Dienstgrad: SS-Sturmmann

Geburtstag: 28.2.26 u. -ort: [redacted]

Todestag: 1.3.45 u. -ort: Vogelsang

Erkenn.-Marke: III./SS-Pz.Gren.Ausb.Rgt. 295
(Vollständige Anschrift angeben)

Anschrift der Angehörigen: Vater:
Hermann Moritz [redacted]
Reideburgerstr. 32

Nationalität des Toten (nur bei Verbündeten oder Feindgefallenen): —

Tod erfolgte a) im Felde (Kriegsschauplatz): Osten
b) im Heimatgebiet (Wehrkreis): —
c) im Ausland (Staat): —

Begräbnisort: Fünfeichen

Gemeinde, Kreis: Guben/ Nieder-Laus.
(Himmelsrichtung und Entfernung von dem nächsten größeren Ort)

~~Ehrenhain~~ Kriegerfriedhof, ~~Gemeindefriedhof~~

Einzelgrab Nr.: ~~5~~ 24

Reihengrab Nr.: — Kameradengrab —

Lage der Grabstätte: 9 km westl. Fürstenberg/ Oder Feld 2 Reihe 5 Nr. 24

Vermerke über den Toten. Getötet durch Feindeinwirkung (Art der Verwundung): Gra. Spl. Kopf —

Unfall, Krankheit, Selbstmord (unbedingt angeben, ob mit oder ohne militärische Ehren beigesetzt) —

Erschießen laut Urteil: —
*) Nichtzutreffendes streichen!

Grab-Lageskizze auf der Rückseite beachten!
Die gestellten Fragen sind möglichst lückenlos und gewissenhaft zu beantworten.
Klare deutliche Schrift!
Truppenteil **und** Feldpostnummer dürfen zusammen angegeben werden.

Das Grab ist vom WGO erfaßt unter der Nr.

2112. 5. 44. Kroll & Straus, Berlin SO 36 – 20000. 12. 44

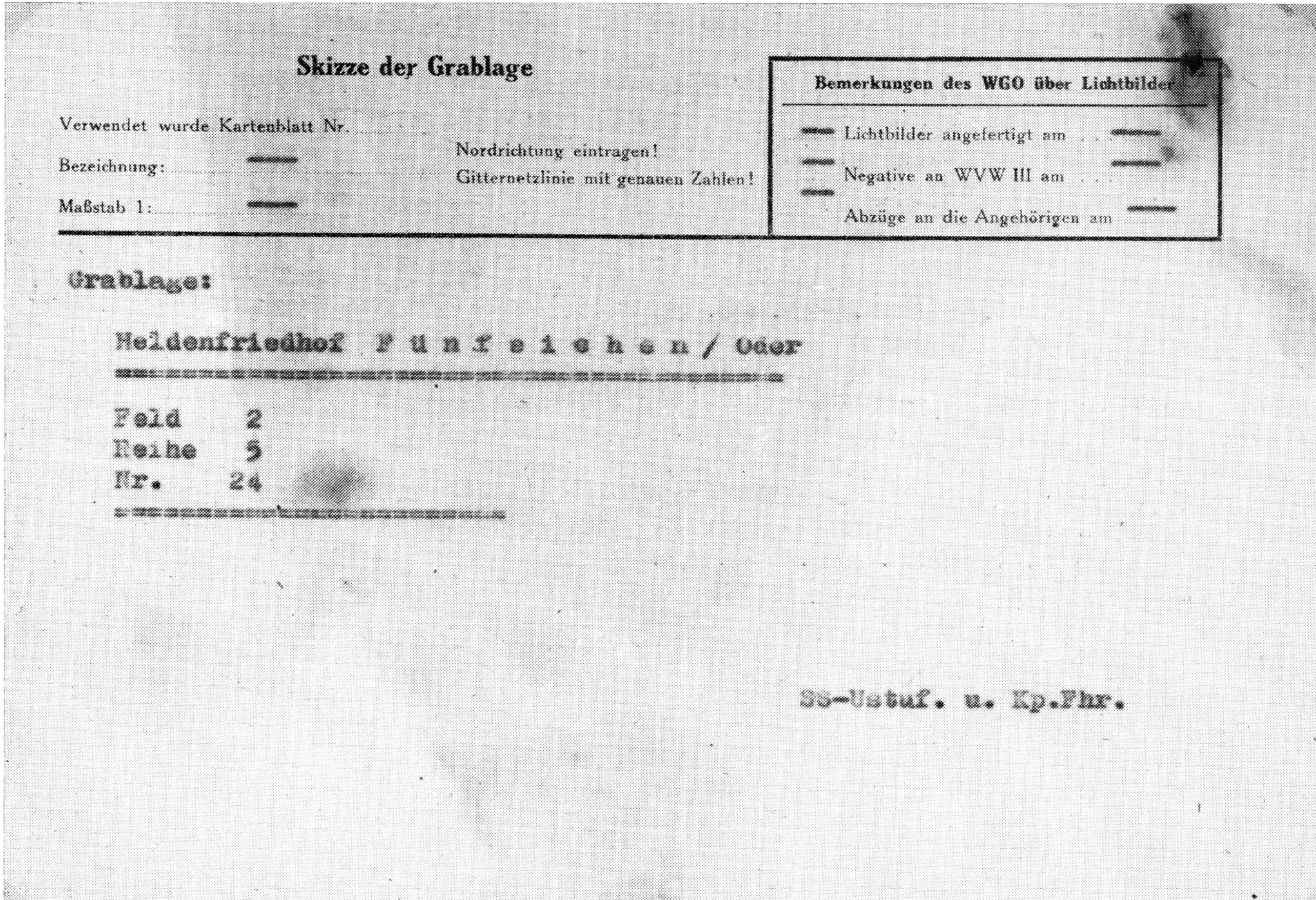

Skizze der Grablage

Verwendet wurde Kartenblatt Nr.

Bezeichnung: ——

Maßstab 1: ——

Nordrichtung eintragen!

Gitternetzlinie mit genauen Zahlen!

Bemerkungen des WGO über Lichtbilder

— Lichtbilder angefertigt am ——

— Negative an WVW III am ——

— Abzüge an die Angehörigen am ——

Grablage:

Heldenfriedhof F ü n f e i c h e n / Oder

Feld 2
Reihe 5
Nr. 24

SS-Ustuf. u. Kp.Fhr.

Dienststelle
F.P.Nr. 26 667 L

O.U., 20.3.45

Gefallenen-Nachlass des
SS-Strm. M o r i t z, Kurt

Briefschaften
1 Paar Hosenträger
Schreibpapier
1 Flasche Pitralon
1 Stück Seife

.d.R.:

SS-Hauptscharführer
u. Stabsscharführer

SS-Untersturmführer
u. Kompanieführer

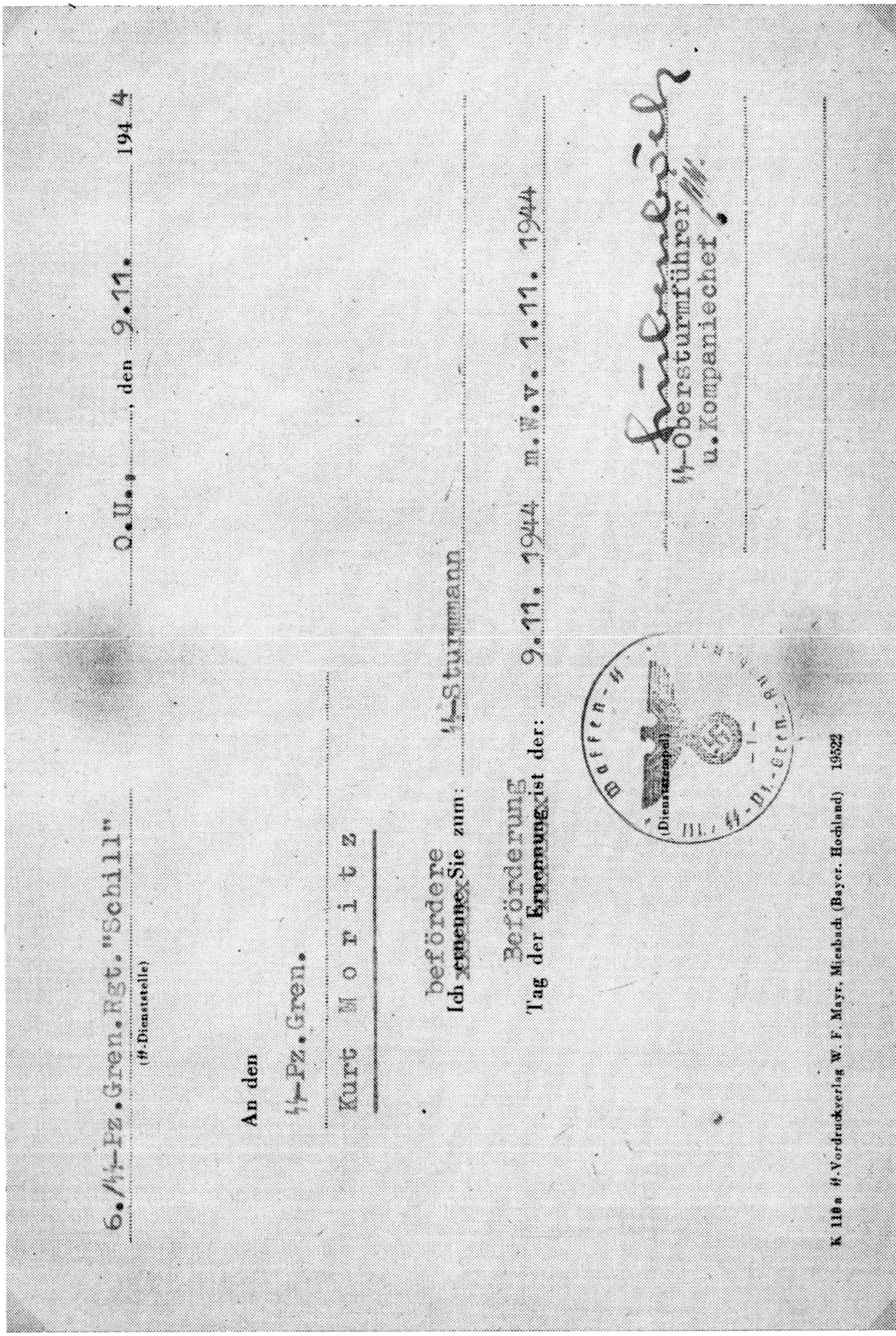

6./SS-Pz.Gren.Rgt."Schill" O.U., den 9.11. 1944
(SS-Dienststelle)

An den
SS-Pz.Gren.
Kurt Moritz

Ich befördere Sie zum: SS-Sturmmann

Tag der Beförderung ist der: 9.11.1944 m.W.v. 1.11.1944

(Dienststempel)

SS-Obersturmführer
u. Kompaniechef

K 118a SS-Vordruckverlag W. F. Mayr, Miesbach (Bayer. Hochland) 19522

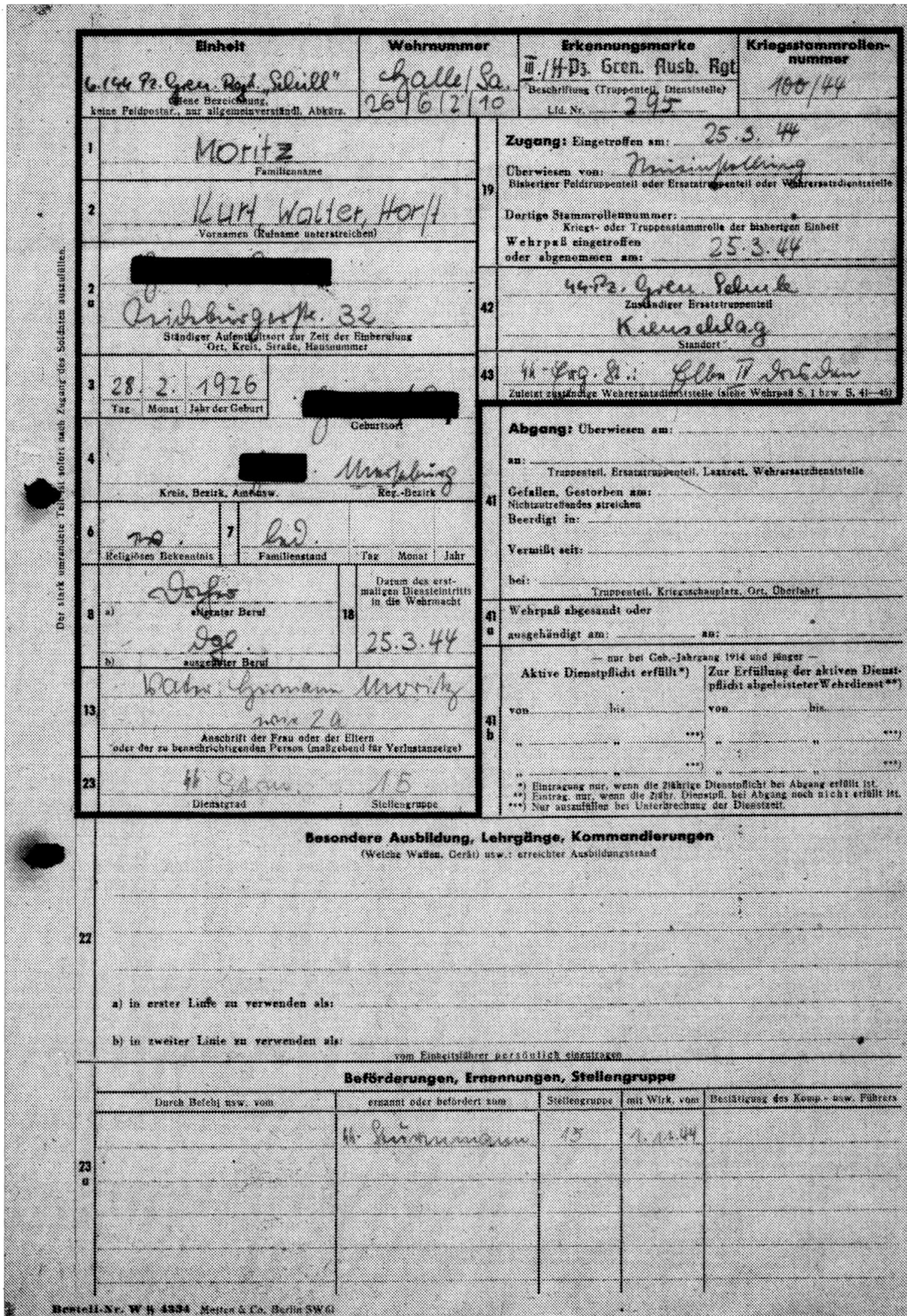

Einheit: 6./44 Pz. Gren. Rgt. „Schill"
(offene Bezeichnung, keine Feldpostnr., nur allgemeinverständl. Abkürz.)

Wehrnummer: Halle/Sa. 26/6/2/10

Erkennungsmarke: III./44-Pz. Gren. Ausb. Rgt.
Beschriftung (Truppenteil, Dienststelle)
Lfd. Nr. 295

Kriegsstammrollennummer: 100/44

1 Moritz
Familienname

2 Kurt, Walter, Horst
Vornamen (Rufname unterstreichen)

2a Friedbürgstr. 32
Ständiger Aufenthaltsort zur Zeit der Einberufung
Ort, Kreis, Straße, Hausnummer

3 28 | 2. | 1926
Tag | Monat | Jahr der Geburt
Geburtsort

4 Kreis, Bezirk, Amt usw. | Merseburg
Reg.-Bezirk

6 Religiöses Bekenntnis | 7 led.
Familienstand | Tag | Monat | Jahr

8 a) erlernter Beruf
b) Dgl.
ausgeübter Beruf

18 Datum des erstmaligen Diensteintritts in die Wehrmacht: 25.3.44

13 Vater: Hermann Moritz
Anschrift der Frau oder der Eltern oder der zu benachrichtigenden Person (maßgebend für Verlustanzeige)

23 44 Gren. | 15
Dienstgrad | Stellengruppe

19 Zugang: Eingetroffen am: 25.3.44
Überwiesen von:
Bisheriger Feldtruppenteil oder Ersatztruppenteil oder Wehrersatzdienststelle
Dortige Stammrollennummer:
Kriegs- oder Truppenstammrolle der bisherigen Einheit
Wehrpaß eingetroffen oder abgenommen am: 25.3.44

42 44 Pz. Gren. Schule
Zuständiger Ersatztruppenteil
Kienschlag
Standort

43 44-Erg. A.: Elbe II Dresden
Zuletzt zuständige Wehrersatzdienststelle (siehe Wehrpaß S. 1 bzw. S. 41—45)

41 Abgang: Überwiesen am:
an:
Truppenteil, Ersatztruppenteil, Lazarett, Wehrersatzdienststelle
Gefallen, Gestorben am:
Nichtzutreffendes streichen
Beerdigt in:
Vermißt seit:
bei:
Truppenteil, Kriegsschauplatz, Ort, Überfahrt

41a Wehrpaß abgesandt oder ausgehändigt am: an:

41b — nur bei Geb.-Jahrgang 1914 und jünger —
Aktive Dienstpflicht erfüllt*) | Zur Erfüllung der aktiven Dienstpflicht abgeleisteter Wehrdienst**)
von ... bis ... | von ... bis ...
*) Eintragung nur, wenn die 2jährige Dienstpflicht bei Abgang erfüllt ist.
**) Eintrag. nur, wenn die 2jähr. Dienstpfl. bei Abgang noch nicht erfüllt ist.
***) Nur ausfüllen bei Unterbrechung der Dienstzeit.

Der stark umrandete Teil ist sofort nach Zugang des Soldaten auszufüllen.

22 Besondere Ausbildung, Lehrgänge, Kommandierungen
(Welche Waffen, Gerät) usw.: erreichter Ausbildungsstand
a) in erster Linie zu verwenden als:
b) in zweiter Linie zu verwenden als:
vom Einheitsführer persönlich einzutragen

23a Beförderungen, Ernennungen, Stellengruppe

Durch Befehl usw. vom	ernannt oder befördert zum	Stellengruppe	mit Wirk. vom	Bestätigung des Komp.- usw. Führers
	44-Sturmmann	15	1.11.44	

Bestell-Nr. W B 4334 Metten & Co. Berlin SW 61

Orden und Ehrenzeichen (auch Auszeichnung durch Namensnennung, z. B. im Bericht des OKW., im Ehrenblatt des deutschen Heeres)

24

Datum	Art der Auszeichnung	Verleihungsurkunde	Bestätigung des Kompanie- usw. Führers
17.10.44	Infanterie Sturmabzeichen Bronze	[illegible] Besitzzeugnis	
4.10.44	Verw. Abz. schwarz	[illegible]	

28

Mitgemachte Schlachten und Gefechte

Datum	Gefechtsbezeichnung *)

*) Einkleben von Umdruckstreifen ist erwünscht. Bei Absendung des Kr. St. Bl. ein Doppel (lose) für das Wehrstammbuch beifügen!

29

Verwundungen und ernstere Erkrankungen, Lazarettaufenthalt

Tag, Monat, Jahr	
21.9.44	Granatsplitter [illegible] Bein

27 a

Kriegsdienstbeschädigungen anerkannt

am (Tag, Monat, Jahr)	Art des Leidens	von welcher Dienststelle

Strafen

24 a *) keine – *) siehe Strafbuchseite

*) Nichtzutreffendes streichen

24 b Strafbuchauszug überwiesen: *) ja – *) nein

24 c **Führung *)**

*) Nur mit folgenden Abstufungen auszudrücken: Vorzüglich, Sehr gut, Ziemlich gut, Genugend, Mangelhaft, Ungenügend.

Dienststempel

Die Richtigkeit bescheinigt:

Datum

Unterschrift des Einheitsführers

Feldpostnummer

Dienstgrad des Einheitsführers

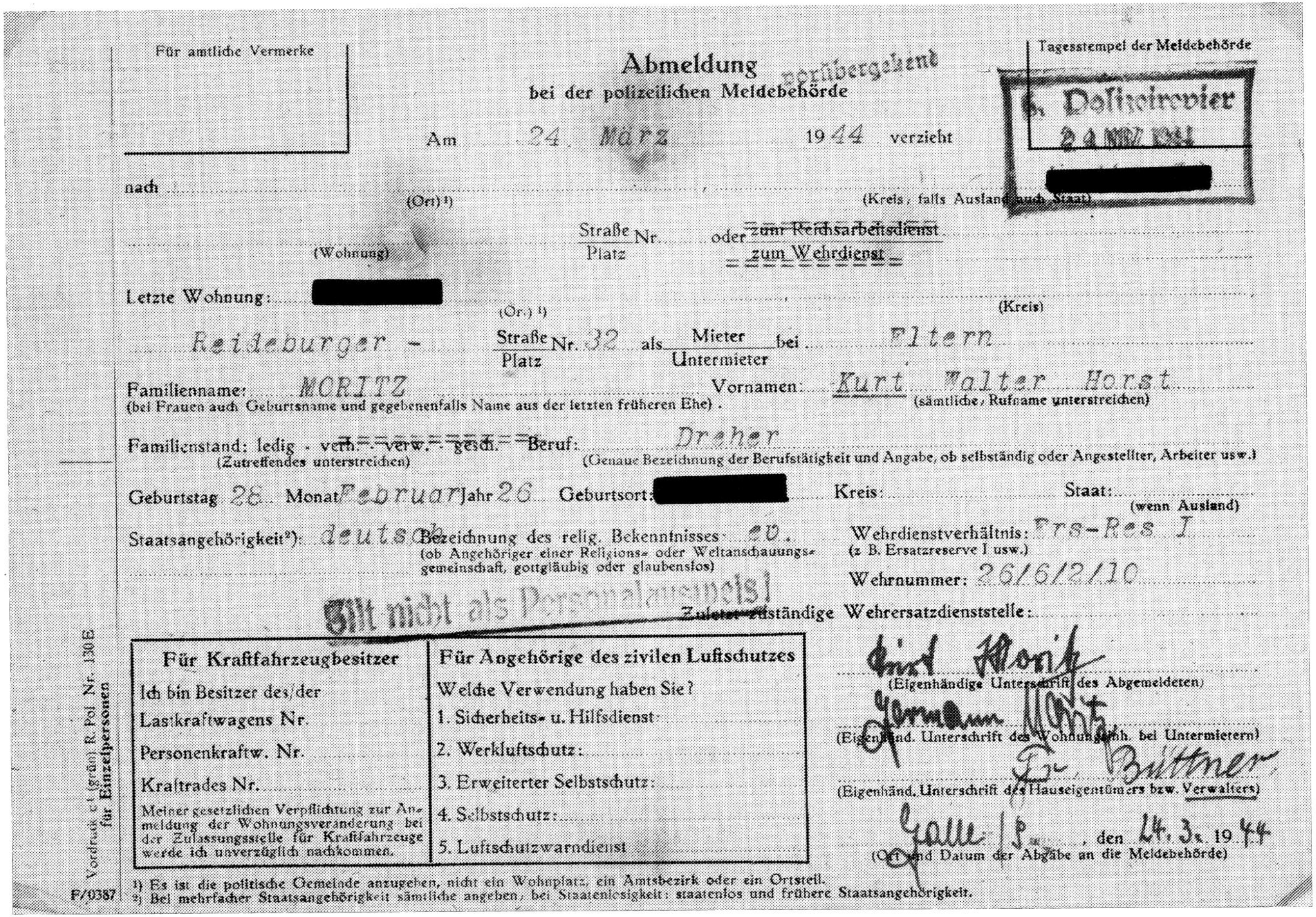

Für amtliche Vermerke

Tagesstempel der Meldebehörde

6. Polizeirevier 24 MÄRZ 1944

Abmeldung vorübergehend

bei der polizeilichen Meldebehörde

Am 24. März 1944 verzieht

nach .... (Ort)[1] .... (Kreis, falls Ausland auch Staat)

.... (Wohnung) Straße/Platz Nr. ...... oder ~~zum Reichsarbeitsdienst~~ zum Wehrdienst

Letzte Wohnung: ████ (Ort)[1] .... (Kreis)

Reideburger – Straße/Platz Nr. 32 als Mieter/Untermieter bei Eltern

Familienname: MORITZ (bei Frauen auch Geburtsname und gegebenenfalls Name aus der letzten früheren Ehe). Vornamen: Kurt Walter Horst (sämtliche, Rufname unterstreichen)

Familienstand: ledig · ~~verh. · verw. · gesch.~~ (Zutreffendes unterstreichen) Beruf: Dreher (Genaue Bezeichnung der Berufstätigkeit und Angabe, ob selbständig oder Angestellter, Arbeiter usw.)

Geburtstag 28 Monat Februar Jahr 26 Geburtsort: ████ Kreis: ...... Staat: ...... (wenn Ausland)

Staatsangehörigkeit[2]): deutsch Bezeichnung des relig. Bekenntnisses: ev. (ob Angehöriger einer Religions- oder Weltanschauungsgemeinschaft, gottgläubig oder glaubenslos) Wehrdienstverhältnis: Ers-Res I (z. B. Ersatzreserve I usw.)

Wehrnummer: 26/6/2/10

Gilt nicht als Personalausweis!

Zuletzt zuständige Wehrersatzdienststelle: ......

Für Kraftfahrzeugbesitzer	Für Angehörige des zivilen Luftschutzes
Ich bin Besitzer des/der	Welche Verwendung haben Sie?
Lastkraftwagens Nr.	1. Sicherheits- u. Hilfsdienst:
Personenkraftw. Nr.	2. Werkluftschutz:
Kraftrades Nr.	3. Erweiterter Selbstschutz:
Meiner gesetzlichen Verpflichtung zur Anmeldung der Wohnungsveränderung bei der Zulassungsstelle für Kraftfahrzeuge werde ich unverzüglich nachkommen.	4. Selbstschutz:
	5. Luftschutzwarndienst

(Eigenhändige Unterschrift des Abgemeldeten)

(Eigenhänd. Unterschrift des Wohnungsinh. bei Untermietern)

(Eigenhänd. Unterschrift des Hauseigentümers bzw. Verwalters)

......, den 24.3. 1944 (Ort und Datum der Abgabe an die Meldebehörde)

1) Es ist die politische Gemeinde anzugeben, nicht ein Wohnplatz, ein Amtsbezirk oder ein Ortsteil.
2) Bei mehrfacher Staatsangehörigkeit sämtliche angeben, bei Staatenlosigkeit: staatenlos und frühere Staatsangehörigkeit.

F/0387 Vordruck c[1] (grün) R. Pol Nr. 130 E für Einzelpersonen

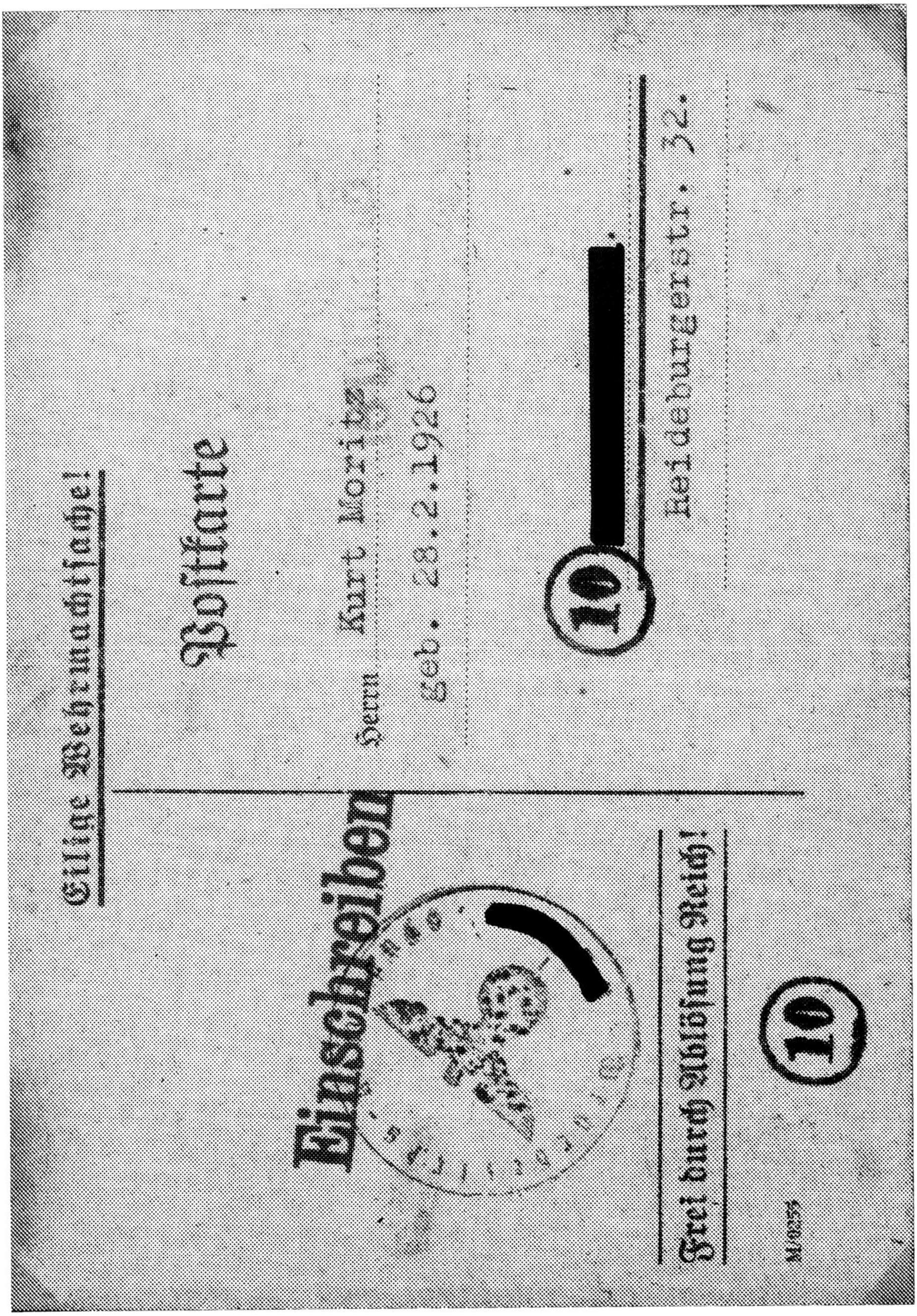
Eilige Wehrmachtsache!
Postkarte
Herrn Kurt Moritz
Geb. 28.2.1926
Heideburgerstr. 32.
Einschreiben
Frei durch Ablösung Reich!
10
10

Der Oberbürgermeister
Ernährungs- und Wirtschaftsamt

Bezirksverteilungsstelle

Abmeldebescheinigung
für den Lebensmittelkartenbezug bei Aufnahme in Gemeinschaftsverpflegung[1] [2]

Abmeldebescheinigung G

Vor- und Zuname: ...

Beruf: ... geb. am 28.2.26

wohnhaft in ... -Straße / Platz Nr. 32

ist heute hier wegen Teilnahme an einer Gemeinschaftsverpflegung für die Zeit vom 25.3. 1944 bis auf weiteres[3]) / bis zum ... 194...[3]) aus der Versorgung mit Lebensmittelkarten abgemeldet worden. Dabei wurden die[3])

1. Lebensmittelkarten einschl. der Zucker-, Marmeladen-, Eierkarten, der Bezugsausweise für entrahmte Frischmilch und für Speisekartoffeln, der Kontrollkarten für besondere Aufrufe und für Fisch, Fischerzeugnisse u. a. abgegeben,
2. Lebensmittelmarken für zusätzliche Lebensmittel abgegeben,
3. Reichskleiderkarte mit ... Abschnitten ... abgegeben / ~~nicht abgegeben~~,
4. Zusatzkleiderkarte für ... mit ... Abschnitten ... abgegeben / ~~nicht abgegeben~~,
5. Reichsseifenkarte ... abgegeben / ~~nicht abgegeben~~,
6. Zusatzseifenkarte ... ~~abgegeben~~ / nicht abgegeben,
7. Tabakkontrollkarte ... ~~abgegeben~~ / nicht abgegeben.
8. ...
9. ...

(Dienststempel) ..., den 24.3. 1944

Im Auftrage: ...
(Unterschrift)

Ich bestätige, daß von mir sämtliche Lebensmittelbedarfsnachweise des oben Genannten — auch die Reichskarte für Marmelade (wahlweise Zucker), die Reichszuckerkarte und die Reichseierkarte —, etwa erhaltene Zusatz- oder Zulagekarten, Lebensmittelmarken usw., ferner die besonderen örtlichen Bezugsausweise usw. wie oben verzeichnet abgegeben worden sind, und daß von der Möglichkeit des Vorgriffs wie folgt Gebrauch gemacht wurde:

1. Reichskarte für Marmelade für ... Wochen vom ... 194 ... bis ... 194
2. Bezugsausweis für Speisekartoffeln durch Einkellerung ... bis ... 194
3. ...

...
(Unterschrift des Abmeldenden)

[1]) [2]) [3]) Siehe Rückseite

024 — 326 — 8. 43. 100 000. L/0353
003 — 5/1 — 8. 56. 43.

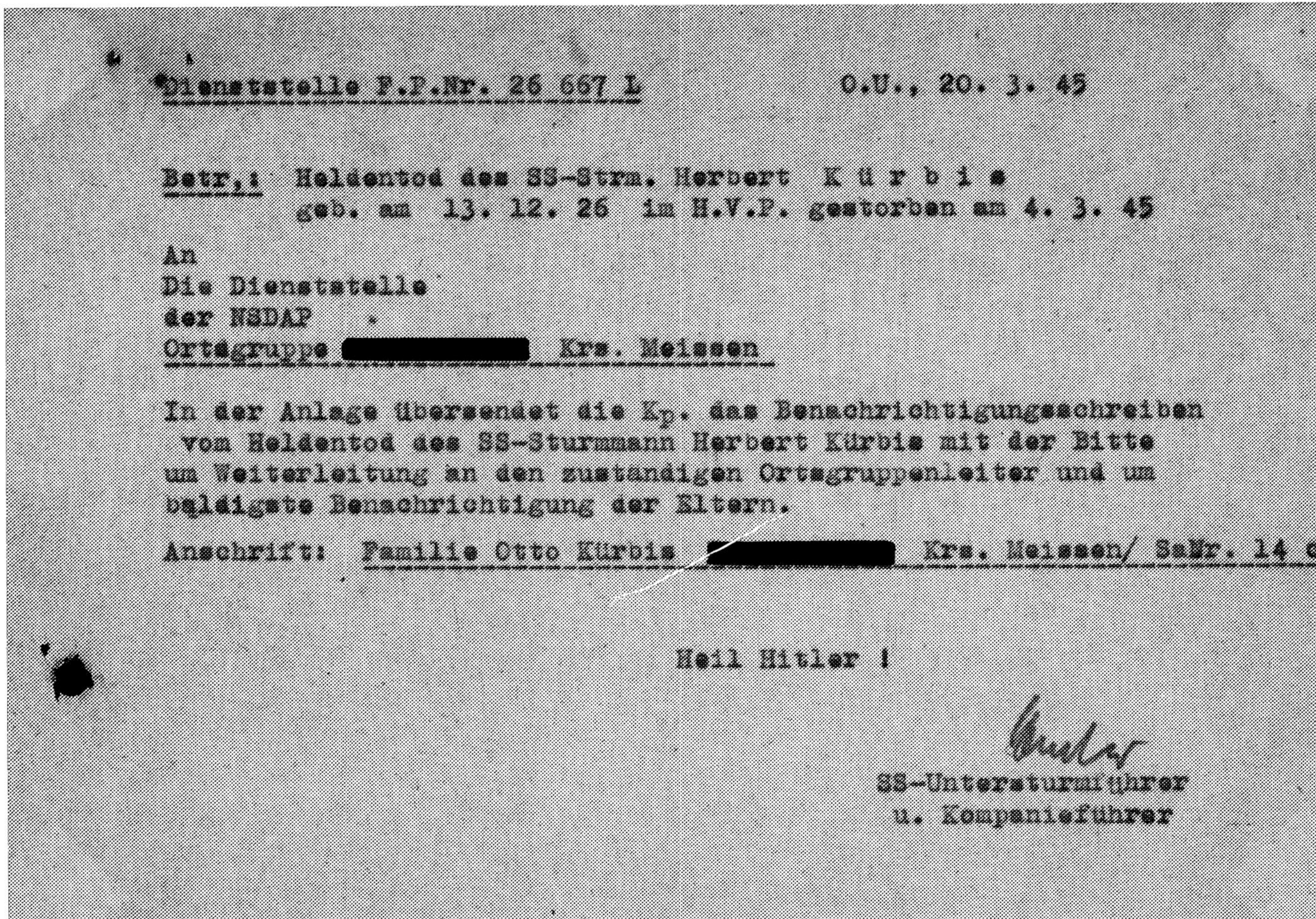

Dienststelle F.P.Nr. 26 667 L   O.U., 20. 3. 45

Betr.: Heldentod des SS-Strm. Herbert K ü r b i s
geb. am 13. 12. 26 im H.V.P. gestorben am 4. 3. 45

An
Die Dienststelle
der NSDAP
Ortsgruppe ██████ Krs. Meissen

In der Anlage übersendet die Kp. das Benachrichtigungsschreiben vom Heldentod des SS-Sturmmann Herbert Kürbis mit der Bitte um Weiterleitung an den zuständigen Ortsgruppenleiter und um baldigste Benachrichtigung der Eltern.

Anschrift: Familie Otto Kürbis ██████ Krs. Meissen/ SaNr. 14 c

Heil Hitler !

SS-Untersturmführer
u. Kompanieführer

Dienststelle
F.P.Nr. 26 667 L

O.U., 20. 3. 45

Familie
Otto K ü r b i s
[redacted] / Krs. Meissen
Nr. 14 c

Sehr geehrte Familie Kürbis !

In meiner Eigenschaft als Kompanie-Führer habe ich die traurige Pflicht Ihnen mitzuteilen, dass Ihr Sohn Herbert bei den Kämpfen um VOGELSANG / Reg.Bez.FRANKFURT/Oder/ am 4. März 1945 schwer verwundet wurde.
Ihr Sohn wurde sofort nach der Verwundung - Granatsplitterverletzung Brust und Oberschenkel - verbunden und nach der Bergung dem Hauptverbandsplatz zugeführt.
Trotz allen ärztlichen Bemühungen ,Ihrem Sohn das Leben zu erhalten verstarb er am gleichen Tage seiner Lazaretteinlieferung im Hauptverbandsplatz.
Es erfüllt mich mit tiefem Bedauern, dass gerade Ihr Sohn Herbert als tapferer, charaktervoller und von allen Kameraden geschätzter Kamerad so früh sein junges Leben lassen musste.
Zugleich im Namen seiner Kameraden spreche ich Ihnen meine wärmste Anteilnahme aus. Die Kompanie wird Ihrem Sohn stets ein ehrendes Andenken bewahren und in ihm ein Vorbild sehen.
Die Gewissheit, dass Ihr Sohn für die Grösse und die Zukunft unseres ewigen Deutschen Volkes sein Leben hingab möge Ihnen in dem schweren Leid, das Sie betroffen hat, Kraft geben und Ihnen ein Trost sein.

In aufrichtigem Mitgefühl
grüsse ich Sie mit

H e i l H i t l e r

[signature]
SS-Untersturmführer
u. Kompanieführer

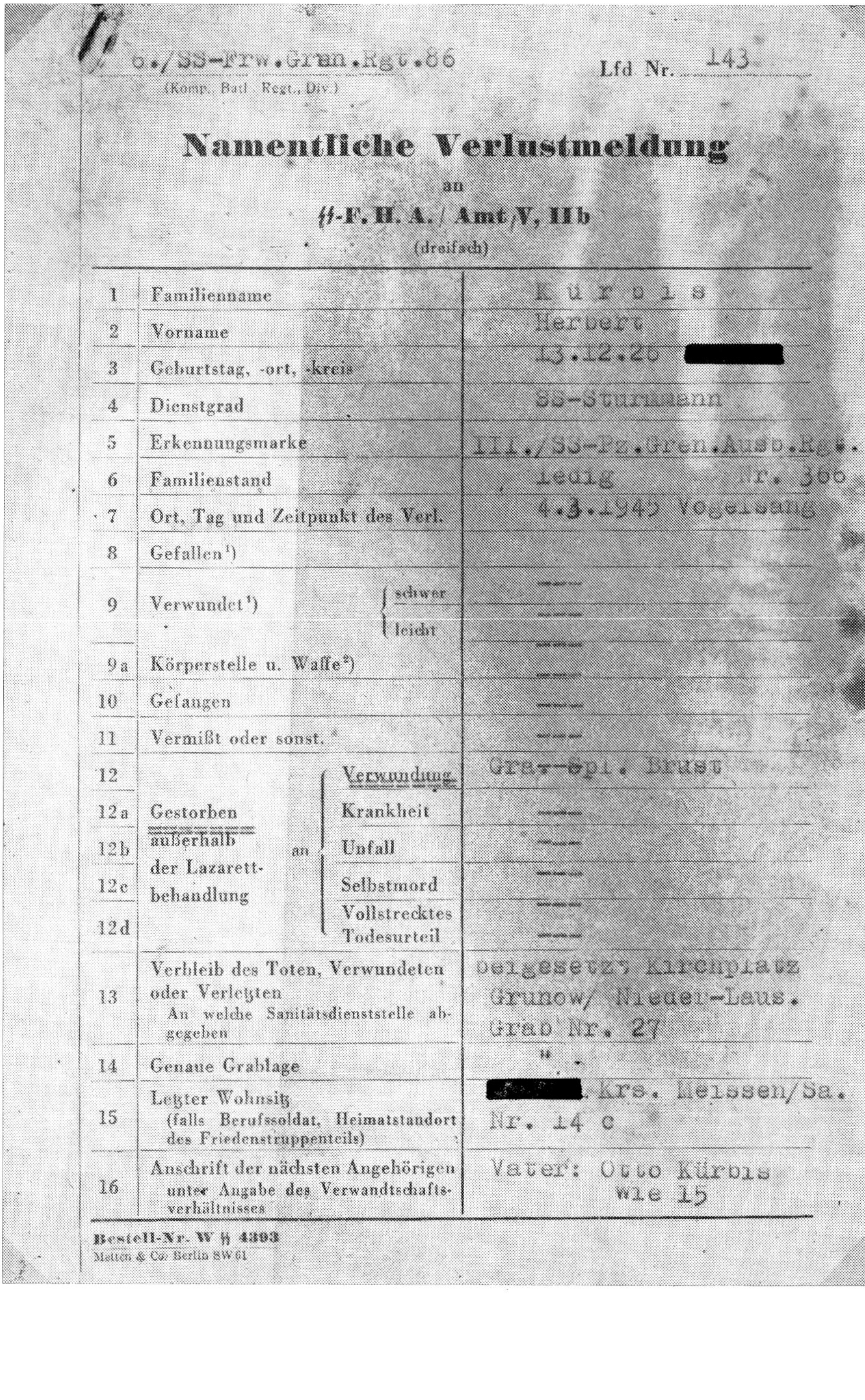

6./SS-Frw.Grun.Rgt.86 Lfd Nr. 143
(Komp., Batl., Regt., Div.)

Namentliche Verlustmeldung
an
SS-F. H. A. / Amt V, IIb
(dreifach)

1	Familienname	K ü r b i s
2	Vorname	Herbert
3	Geburtstag, -ort, -kreis	13.12.26 ███
4	Dienstgrad	SS-Sturmmann
5	Erkennungsmarke	III./SS-Pz.Gren.Ausb.Rgt.
6	Familienstand	ledig Nr. 366
7	Ort, Tag und Zeitpunkt des Verl.	4.3.1945 Vogelsang
8	Gefallen[1])	
9	Verwundet[1]) schwer	----
	leicht	----
9a	Körperstelle u. Waffe[2])	----
10	Gefangen	----
11	Vermißt oder sonst.	----
12	Gestorben außerhalb der Lazarettbehandlung an Verwundung	Gra.-Spl. Brust
12a	Krankheit	----
12b	Unfall	----
12c	Selbstmord	----
12d	Vollstrecktes Todesurteil	----
13	Verbleib des Toten, Verwundeten oder Verletzten An welche Sanitätsdienststelle abgegeben	beigesetzt Kirchplatz Grunow/ Nieder-Laus. Grab Nr. 27
14	Genaue Grablage	"
15	Letzter Wohnsitz (falls Berufssoldat, Heimatstandort des Friedenstruppenteils)	███ Krs. Meissen/Sa. Nr. 14 c
16	Anschrift der nächsten Angehörigen unter Angabe des Verwandtschaftsverhältnisses	Vater: Otto Kürbis wie 15

Bestell-Nr. W SS 4393
Metten & Co. Berlin SW 61

17	Angehörige benachrichtigt	20. 3. 45
18	Staatsangehörigkeit	D.R.
19	Volkszugehörigkeit	
20	Einberufen durch ᛋᛋ-Erg.-Stelle	SS-Erg. St. El[illegible]
21	Eintritt in die Waffen-ᛋᛋ	25. 3. 1945
22		
23		
24		

SS-Ustuf. u. Kp. Fhr.
(Unterschrift)

Raum für Skizze und Kampfbericht bei Vermißten oder Gefangenen

Grablage: Kirchplatz Grunow/ Niederlaus.

Grab Nr. 27

1) Abkürzungen: K. = Kopf, H. = Hals, Br. = Brust, Ba. = Bauch, R. = Rücken, l. A. = linker Arm, (I.G. = Inf.-Gesch., H.Gr. = Handgranaten-Verl., Gs.V. = Kampfstoffvergiftung, A.G. = Art.Gesch.).

2) Hierzu rechnen auch Verstauchung und Verrenkung durch stumpfe Gewalt infolge feindlicher Einwirkung, durch Verschüttung usw.

San.Komp.der 32. SS-Freiw.Gren.Div.
" 3o. Januar "
H.V.P. Grunow

G r u n o w , den 4.3.45

Betr.: SS-Strmm. Herbert K ü r b i s
Bezug: - . -
Anlg.: 1 halbe Erkennungsmarke, 1 Armbanduhr, 1 Mundharmonika, 1 Pfeiffenreiniger, 1 Skizze über Grablage

An die

6./ SS-Freiw.Gren.Regt. " Schill "

Die Dienststelle der San.Komp, der 32. SS-Freiw.Gren.Div. " 3o. Januar " H.V.P. Grunow übersendet in der Anlage 1 halbe Erkennungsmarke, sowie den Nachlass von dem am 4.3.45 gegen lo,55 auf dem H.V.P. Grunow verstorbenen SS-Strmm. Herbert Kürbis.
Soldbuch trug der Verstorbene bei seiner Einlieferung in den H.V.P. nicht bei sich. Das über ihn hier Bekannte stammt aus seinen eigenen Angaben.
SS-Strmm. Herbert Kürbis wurde am 4.3.45 um 16 Uhr auf dem Kirchplatz in Grunow unter militärischen Ehren in Grab 27 beerdigt.

SS-Hauptsturmführer und Zugführer

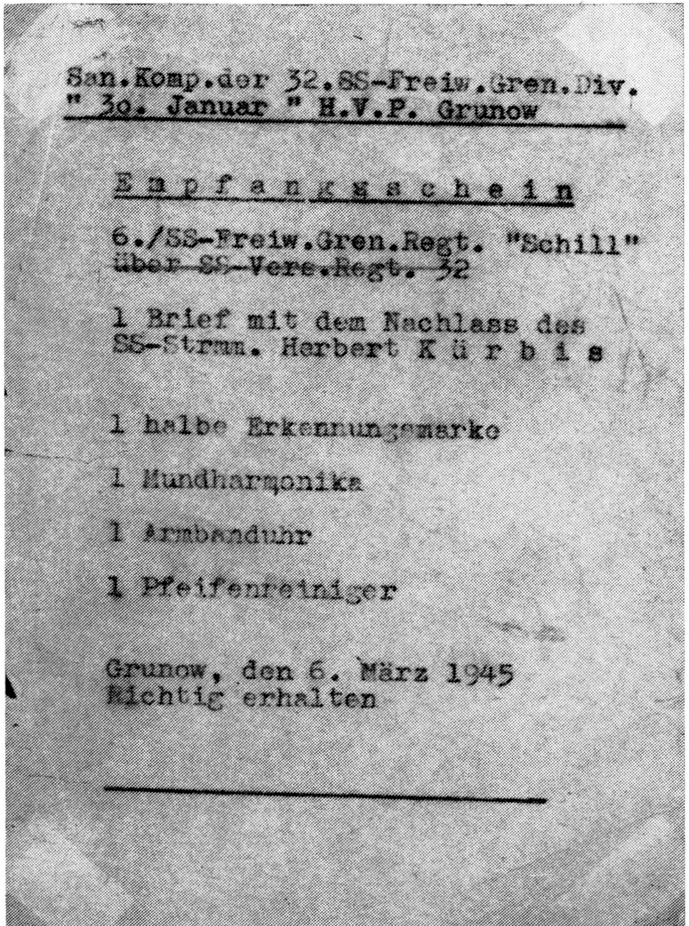

San.Komp.der 32.SS-Freiw.Gren.Div.
" 3o. Januar " H.V.P. Grunow

E m p f a n g s s c h e i n

6./SS-Freiw.Gren.Regt. "Schill"
~~über SS-Vers.Regt. 32~~

1 Brief mit dem Nachlass des
SS-Strmn. Herbert K ü r b i s

1 halbe Erkennungsmarke

1 Mundharmonika

1 Armbanduhr

1 Pfeifenreiniger

Grunow, den 6. März 1945
Richtig erhalten

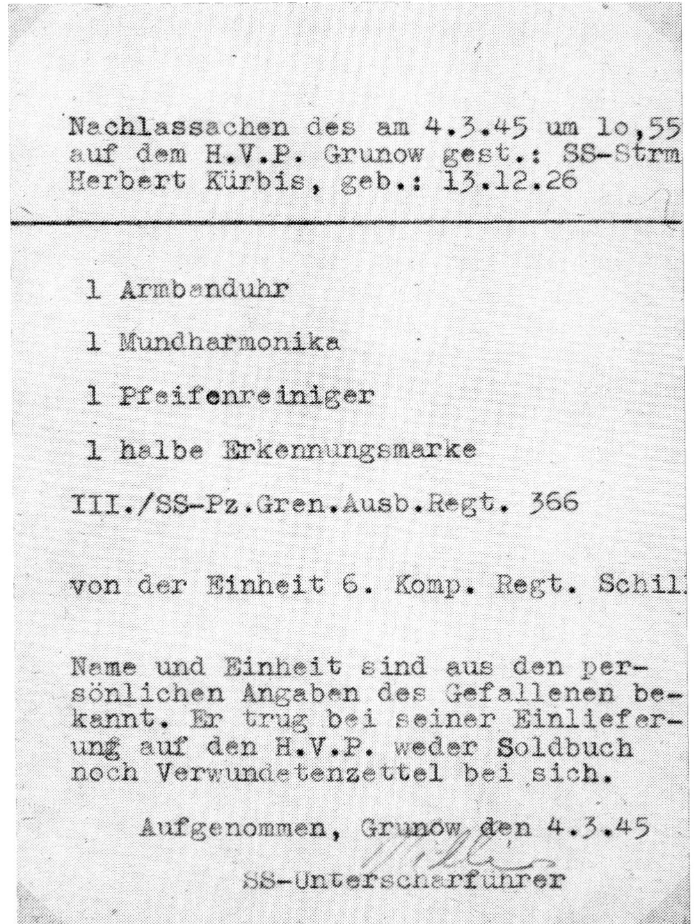

Nachlassachen des am 4.3.45 um 1o,55
auf dem H.V.P. Grunow gest.: SS-Strm
Herbert Kürbis, geb.: 13.12.26

1 Armbanduhr

1 Mundharmonika

1 Pfeifenreiniger

1 halbe Erkennungsmarke

III./SS-Pz.Gren.Ausb.Regt. 366

von der Einheit 6. Komp. Regt. Schil

Name und Einheit sind aus den persönlichen Angaben des Gefallenen bekannt. Er trug bei seiner Einlieferung auf den H.V.P. weder Soldbuch noch Verwundetenzettel bei sich.

Aufgenommen, Grunow den 4.3.45

SS-Unterscharführer

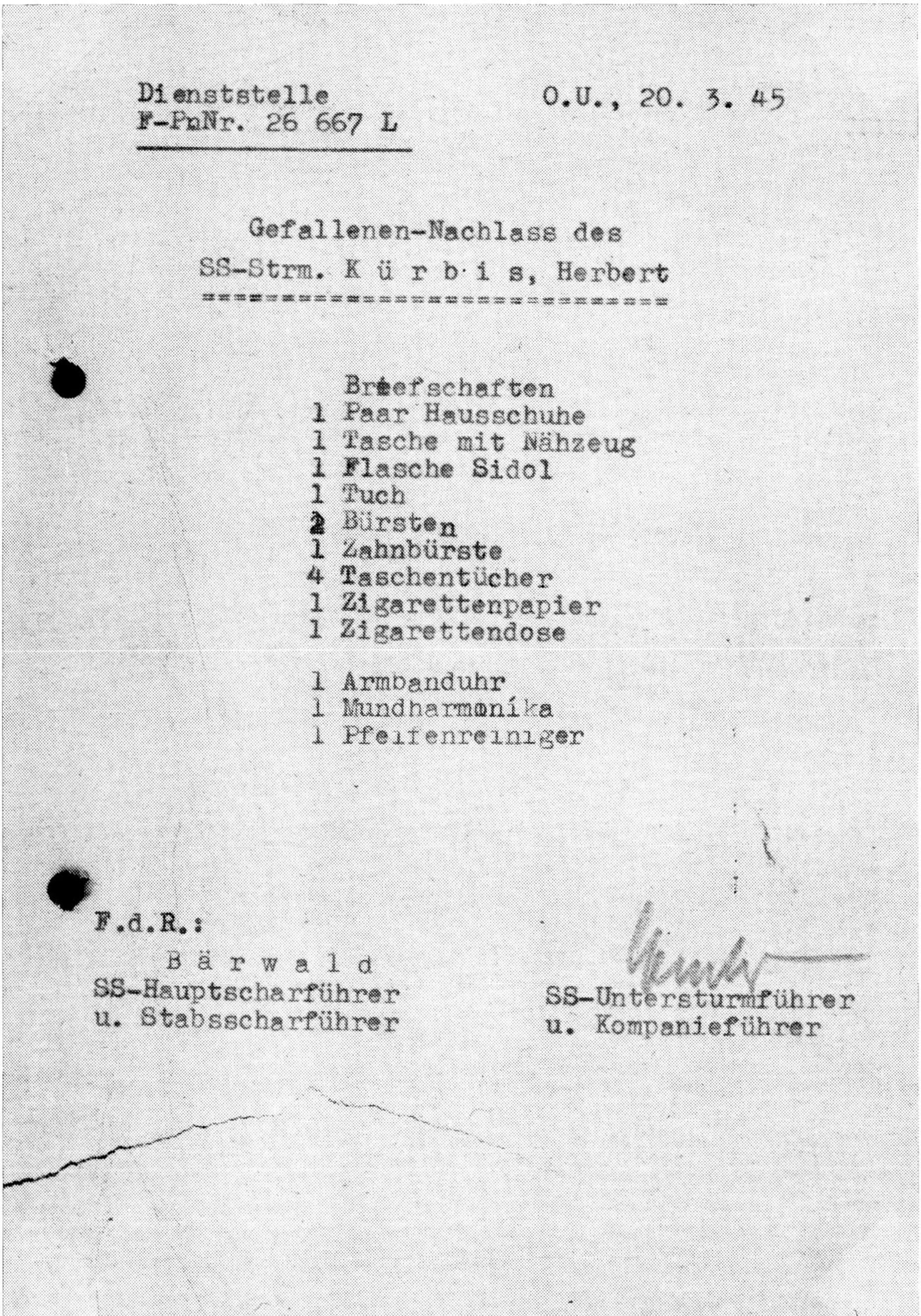

Dienststelle O.U., 20. 3. 45
F-PuNr. 26 667 L

Gefallenen-Nachlass des
SS-Strm. K ü r b i s, Herbert

Briefschaften
1 Paar Hausschuhe
1 Tasche mit Nähzeug
1 Flasche Sidol
1 Tuch
2 Bürsten
1 Zahnbürste
4 Taschentücher
1 Zigarettenpapier
1 Zigarettendose

1 Armbanduhr
1 Mundharmonika
1 Pfeifenreiniger

F.d.R.:
B ä r w a l d
SS-Hauptscharführer
u. Stabsscharführer

SS-Untersturmführer
u. Kompanieführer

Dienststelle
F.P.Nr. 26 667 L

O.U., 20.3.45

Gefallenen-Nachlass des
SS-Strm. Herbert K ü r b i s

3 Tuben Zahnpasta
2 Zahnbürsten
1 Stück Seife m. Seifendose
1 Hemd
1 Paar Strümpfe
2 Taschentücher
1 Halstuch
Schreibpapier
1 Handbürste

F.d.R.:

SS-Hauptscharführer
u. Stabsscharführer

SS-Untersturmführer
u. Kompanieführer

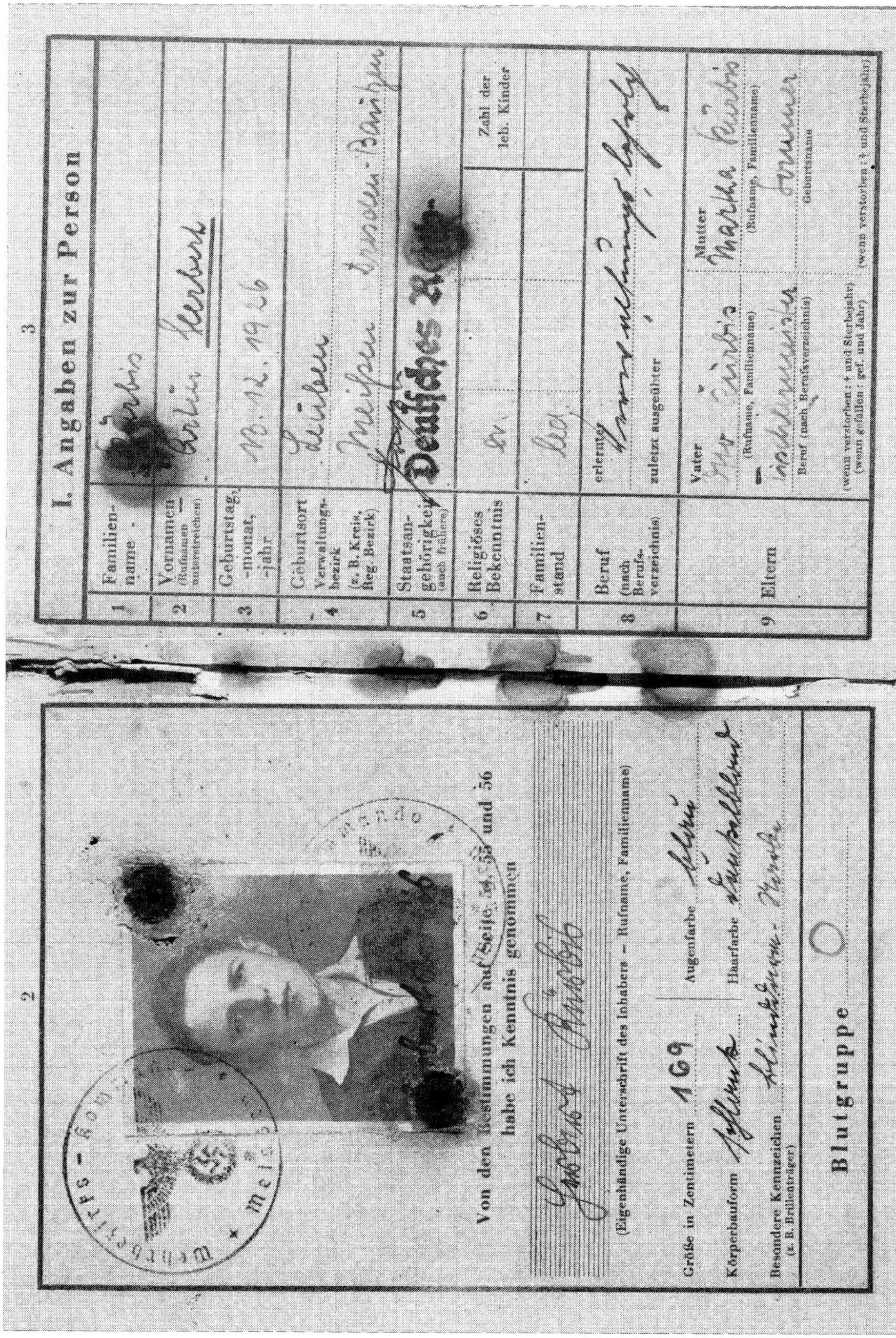
2
Wehrbezirks-Kommando
Meißen
Von den Bestimmungen auf Seite 54, 55 und 56
habe ich Kenntnis genommen
(Eigenhändige Unterschrift des Inhabers – Rufname, Familienname)
Größe in Zentimetern 169
Augenfarbe
Haarfarbe
Körperbauform
Besondere Kennzeichen
(z. B. Brillenträger)
Blutgruppe
3
I. Angaben zur Person
1 Familien-name
2 Vornamen (Rufnamen unterstreichen)
3 Geburtstag, -monat, -jahr
4 Geburtsort Verwaltungsbezirk (z. B. Kreis, Reg. Bezirk)
5 Staatsangehörigkeit (auch frühere)
Deutsches Reich
6 Religiöses Bekenntnis
7 Familienstand
Zahl der leb. Kinder
8 Beruf (nach Berufsverzeichnis)
erlernter
zuletzt ausgeübter
9 Eltern
Vater
Mutter
(Rufname, Familienname)
Beruf (nach Berufsverzeichnis)
Geburtsname
(wenn verstorben: † und Sterbejahr)
(wenn gefallen: gef. und Jahr)

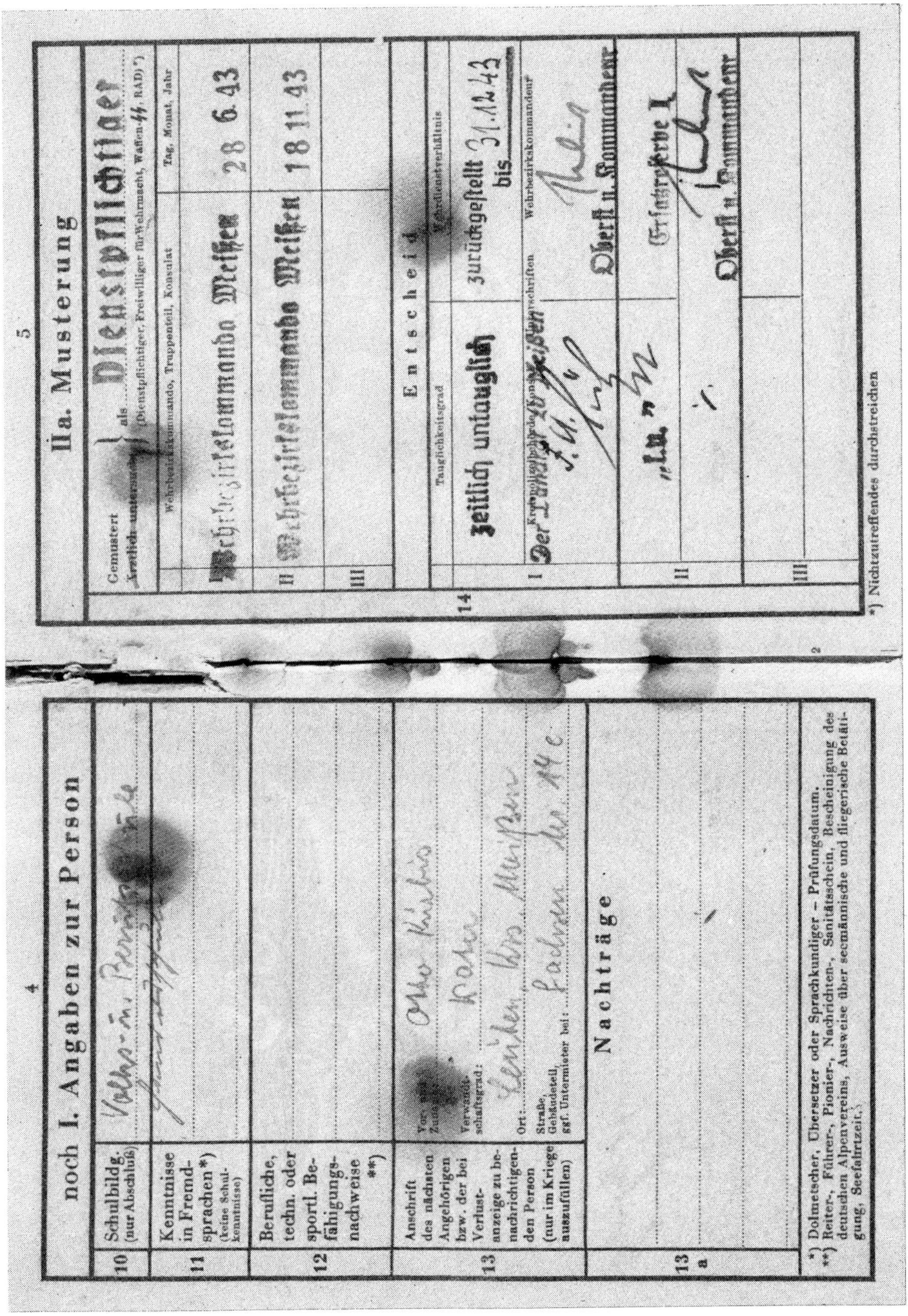

4

noch I. Angaben zur Person

10	Schulbildg. (nur Abschluß)	Volks- u. Berufsschule
11	Kenntnisse in Fremdsprachen*) (keine Schulkenntnisse)	
12	Berufliche, techn. oder sportl. Befähigungsnachweise **)	
13	Anschrift des nächsten Angehörigen bzw. der bei Verlustanzeige zu benachrichtigenden Person (nur im Kriege auszufüllen)	Vor- und Zuname: Otto Kubis Verwandtschaftsgrad: Vater Ort: Zehren Kr. Meißen Straße, Gebäudeteil, ggf. Untermieter bei: ...

Nachträge

13 a

*) Dolmetscher, Übersetzer oder Sprachkundiger – Prüfungsdatum.
**) Reiter-, Führer-, Pionier-, Nachrichten-, Sanitätsschein, Bescheinigung des deutschen Alpenvereins, Ausweise über seemännische und fliegerische Betätigung, Seefahrtzeit.

5

IIa. Musterung

Gemustert / ärztlich untersucht als Dienstpflichtiger (Dienstpflichtiger, Freiwilliger für Wehrmacht, Waffen-SS, RAD)*)

	Wehrbezirkskommando, Truppenteil, Konsulat	Tag, Monat, Jahr
I	Wehrbezirkskommando Meißen	28.6.43
II	Wehrbezirkskommando Meißen	18.11.43
III		

14 **Entscheid**

	Tauglichkeitsgrad	Wehrdienstverhältnis
I	zeitlich untauglich	zurückgestellt bis 31.12.43
	Kreispolizeibehörde / Unterschriften: Der Landrat zu Meißen i.A.	Wehrbezirkskommandeur: Oberst u. Kommandeur
II	„tu."	Ersatzreserve I Oberst u. Kommandeur
III		

*) Nichtzutreffendes durchstreichen

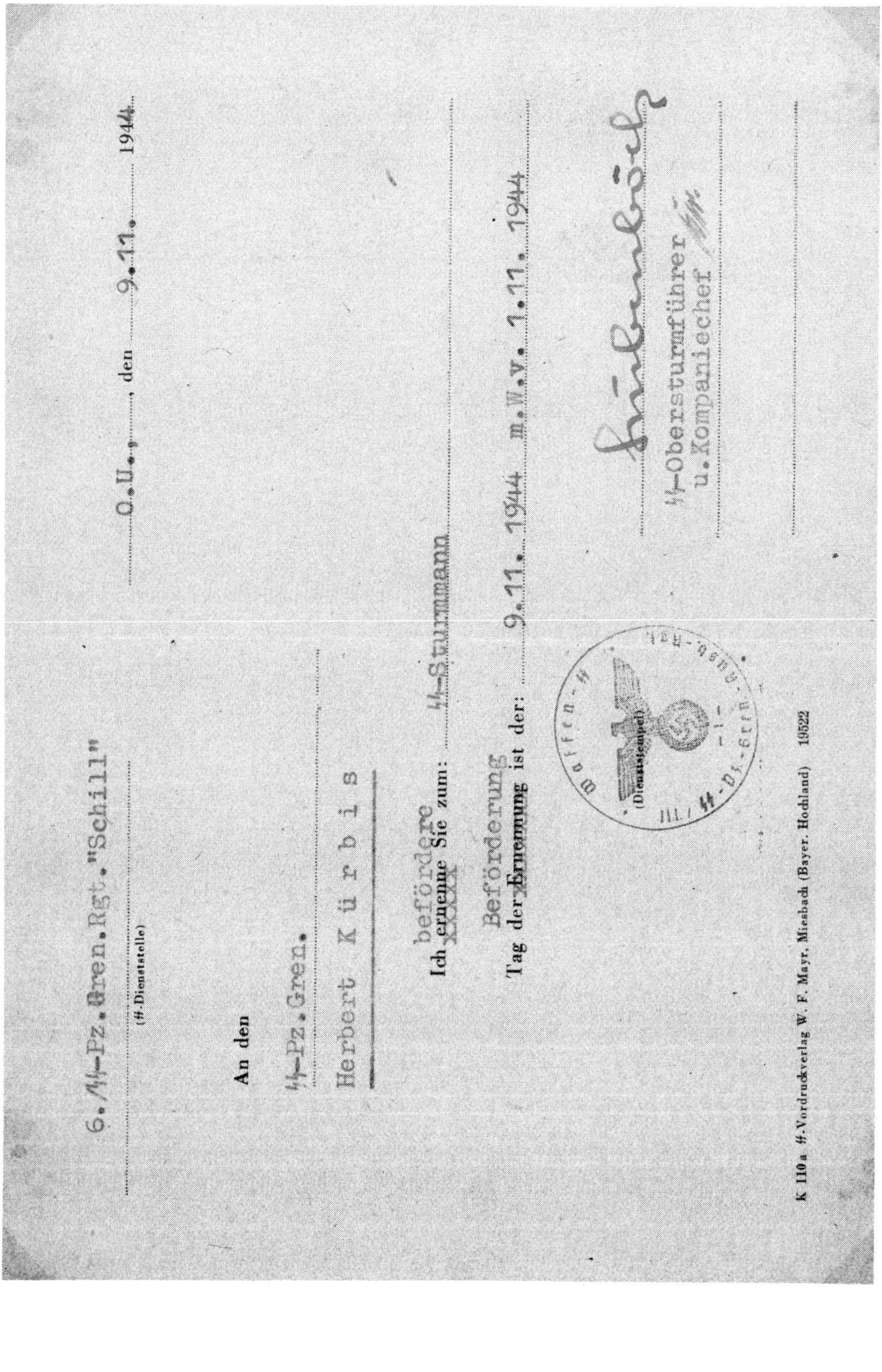
6. SS-Pz.Gren.Rgt. "Schill"
(SS-Dienststelle)

O.U., den 9.11. 1944

An den
SS-Pz.Gren.
Herbert Kürbis

Ich ~~ernenne~~ befördere Sie zum: SS-Sturmmann

Tag der ~~Ernennung~~ Beförderung ist der: 9.11.1944 m.W.v. 1.11.1944

(Dienststempel)

SS-Obersturmführer
u. Kompaniechef

K 110a SS-Vordruckverlag W. F. Mayr, Miesbach (Bayer. Hochland) 19522

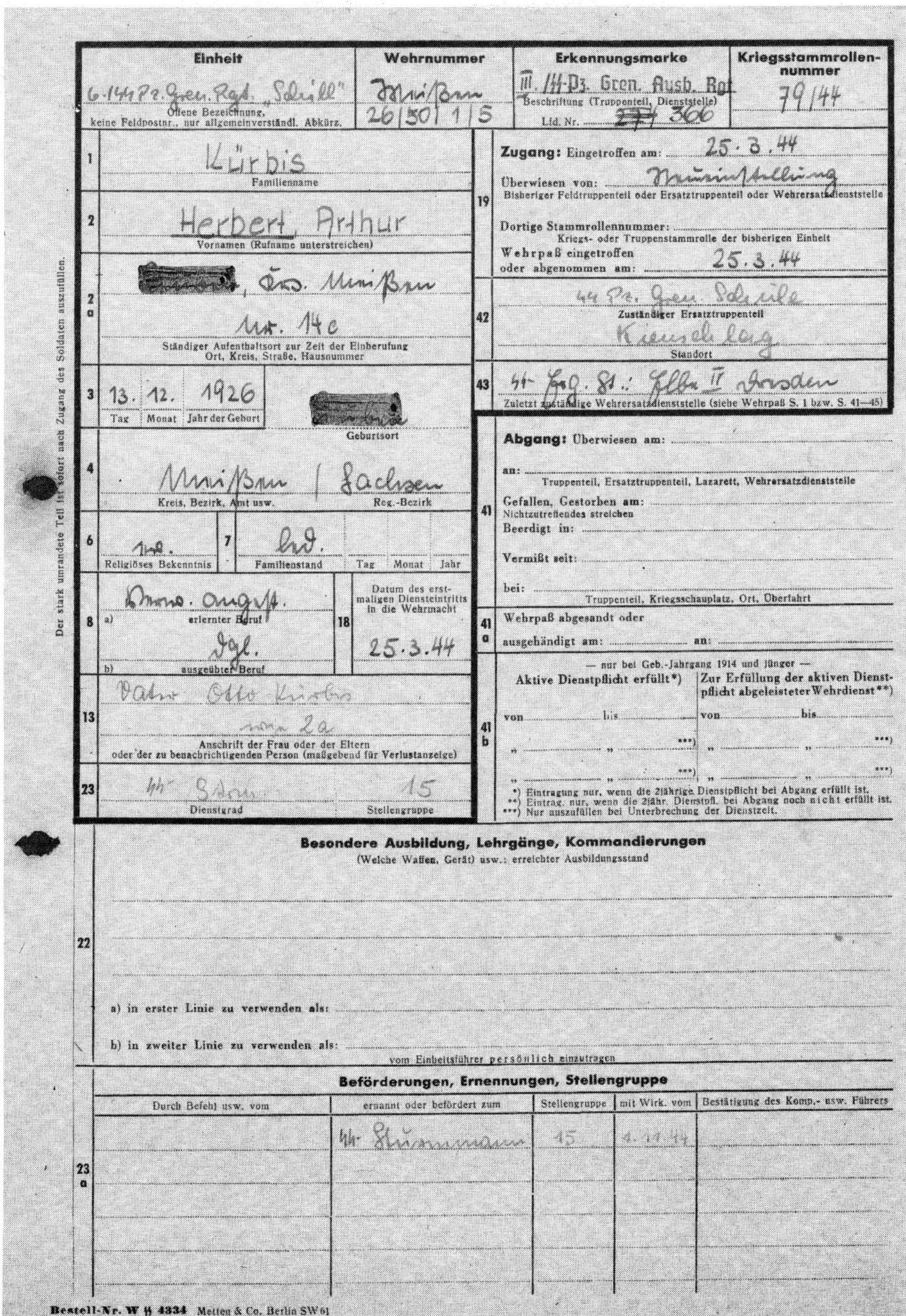

Einheit	Wehrnummer	Erkennungsmarke	Kriegsstammrollennummer
6./44 Pz. Gren. Rgt. „Schill" — Offene Bezeichnung, keine Feldpostnr., nur allgemeinverständl. Abkürz.	Meißen 26/50/1/5	III. SS-Pz. Gren. Ausb. Rgt. — Beschriftung (Truppenteil, Dienststelle) — Lfd. Nr. 366	79/44

1 Kürbis — Familienname

2 Herbert Arthur — Vornamen (Rufname unterstreichen)

2a [redacted], Krs. Meißen, Nr. 14c — Ständiger Aufenthaltsort zur Zeit der Einberufung Ort, Kreis, Straße, Hausnummer

3 13. 12. 1926 — Tag, Monat, Jahr der Geburt — [redacted] — Geburtsort

4 Meißen / Sachsen — Kreis, Bezirk, Amt usw. — Reg.-Bezirk

6 ev. — Religiöses Bekenntnis — 7 led. — Familienstand — Tag, Monat, Jahr

8 a) Kraus. angest. — erlernter Beruf — b) dgl. — ausgeübter Beruf

18 Datum des erstmaligen Diensteintritts in die Wehrmacht: 25.3.44

13 Vater Otto Kürbis wie 2a — Anschrift der Frau oder der Eltern oder der zu benachrichtigenden Person (maßgebend für Verlustanzeige)

23 SS-Schtz. — Dienstgrad — 15 — Stellengruppe

19 **Zugang:** Eingetroffen am: 25. 3. 44
Überwiesen von: Musterung
Bisheriger Feldtruppenteil oder Ersatztruppenteil oder Wehrersatzdienststelle
Dortige Stammrollennummer: — Kriegs- oder Truppenstammrolle der bisherigen Einheit
Wehrpaß eingetroffen oder abgenommen am: 25. 3. 44

42 SS Pz. Gren. Schule — Zuständiger Ersatztruppenteil — Kienschlag — Standort

43 SS-Erg. St.: Elbe II Dresden — Zuletzt zuständige Wehrersatzdienststelle (siehe Wehrpaß S. 1 bzw. S. 41—45)

41 **Abgang:** Überwiesen am:
an: — Truppenteil, Ersatztruppenteil, Lazarett, Wehrersatzdienststelle
Gefallen, Gestorben am: — Nichtzutreffendes streichen
Beerdigt in:
Vermißt seit:
bei: — Truppenteil, Kriegsschauplatz, Ort, Überfahrt

41a Wehrpaß abgesandt oder ausgehändigt am: an:

41b — nur bei Geb.-Jahrgang 1914 und jünger —
Aktive Dienstpflicht erfüllt*) von bis „ „ ***) „ „ ***)
Zur Erfüllung der aktiven Dienstpflicht abgeleisteter Wehrdienst**) von bis „ „ ***) „ „ ***)
*) Eintragung nur, wenn die 2jährige Dienstpflicht bei Abgang erfüllt ist.
**) Eintrag. nur, wenn die 2jähr. Dienstpfl. bei Abgang noch nicht erfüllt ist.
***) Nur auszufüllen bei Unterbrechung der Dienstzeit.

22 **Besondere Ausbildung, Lehrgänge, Kommandierungen**
(Welche Waffen, Gerät) usw.: erreichter Ausbildungsstand
a) in erster Linie zu verwenden als:
b) in zweiter Linie zu verwenden als:
vom Einheitsführer persönlich einzutragen

23a **Beförderungen, Ernennungen, Stellengruppe**

Durch Befehl usw. vom	ernannt oder befördert zum	Stellengruppe	mit Wirk. vom	Bestätigung des Komp.- usw. Führers
	SS-Sturmmann	15	1.11.44	

Der stark umrandete Teil ist sofort nach Zugang des Soldaten auszufüllen.

Bestell-Nr. W SS 4334 Metten & Co. Berlin SW 61

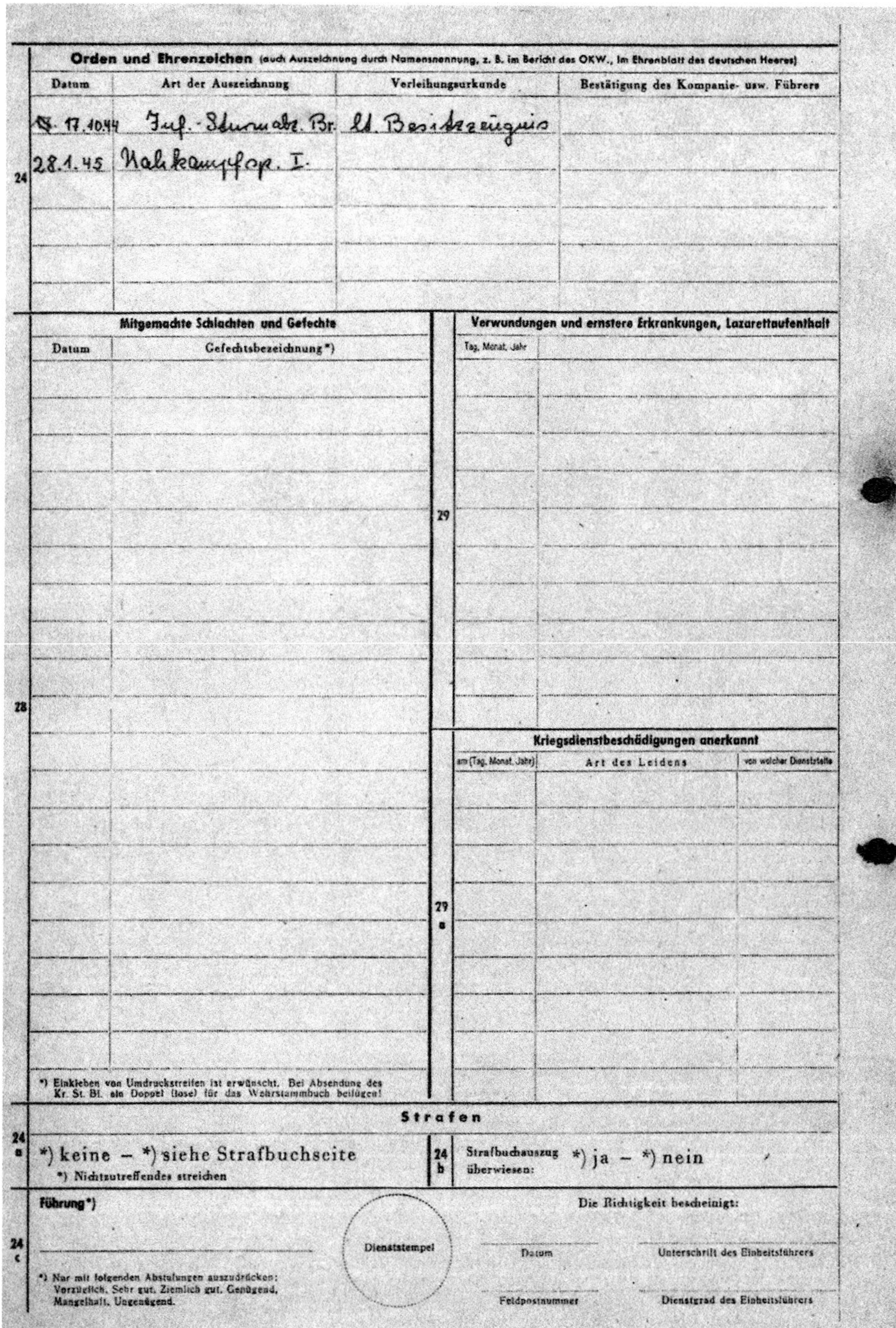

Orden und Ehrenzeichen (auch Auszeichnung durch Namensnennung, z. B. im Bericht des OKW., im Ehrenblatt des deutschen Heeres)

	Datum	Art der Auszeichnung	Verleihungsurkunde	Bestätigung des Kompanie- usw. Führers
24	17.10.44	Inf.-Sturmabz. Br.	Besitzzeugnis	
	28.1.45	Nahkampfsp. I.		

Mitgemachte Schlachten und Gefechte (28)

Datum	Gefechtsbezeichnung *)

*) Einkleben von Umdruckstreifen ist erwünscht. Bei Absendung des Kr. St. Bl. als Doppel (lose) für das Wehrstammbuch beifügen!

Verwundungen und ernstere Erkrankungen, Lazarettaufenthalt (29)

Tag, Monat, Jahr	

Kriegsdienstbeschädigungen anerkannt (29 a)

am (Tag, Monat, Jahr)	Art des Leidens	von welcher Dienststelle

Strafen

24 a *) keine – *) siehe Strafbuchseite

*) Nichtzutreffendes streichen

24 b Strafbuchauszug überwiesen: *) ja – *) nein

24 c **Führung *)**

*) Nur mit folgenden Abstufungen auszudrücken: Vorzüglich, Sehr gut, Ziemlich gut, Genügend, Mangelhaft, Ungenügend.

Dienststempel

Die Richtigkeit bescheinigt:

Datum — Unterschrift des Einheitsführers

Feldpostnummer — Dienstgrad des Einheitsführers

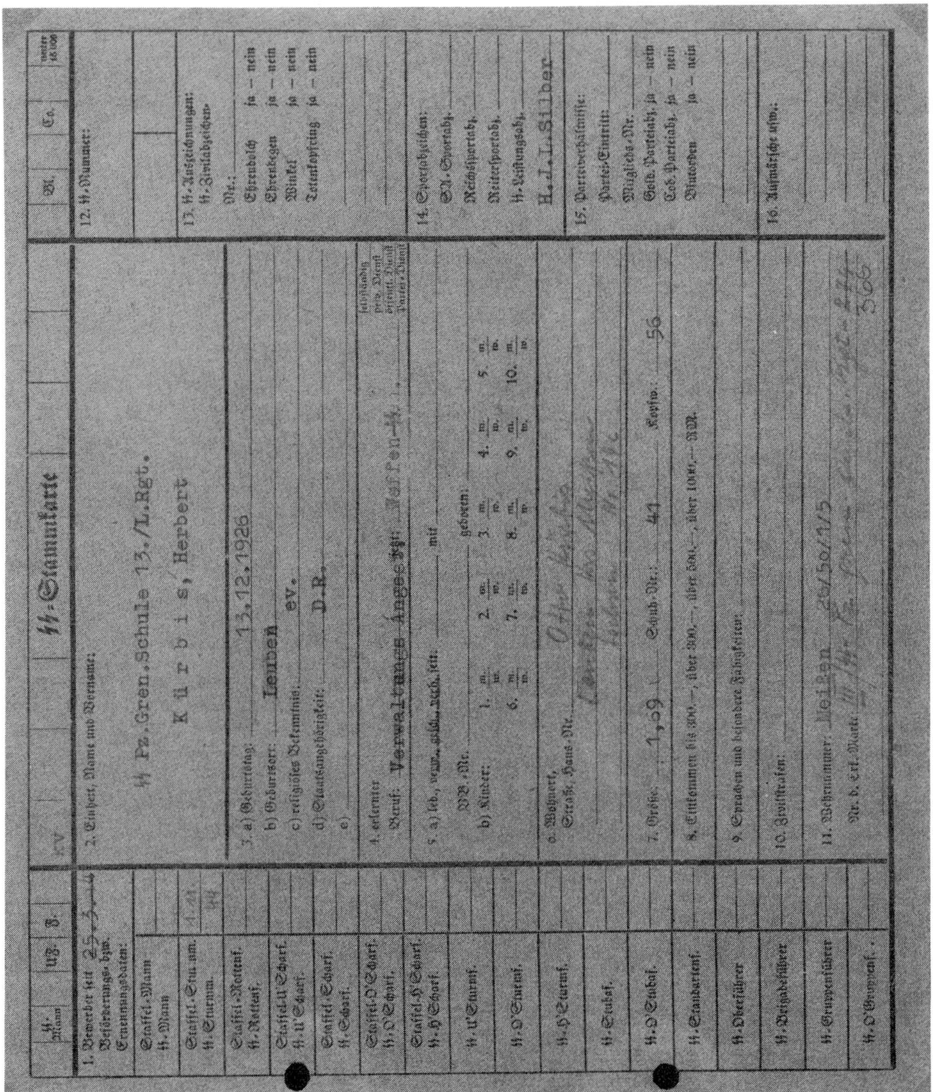

SS-Stammkarte

1. Bewerber seit
Beförderungs- bzw. Ernennungsdaten:

Staffel-Mann / SS-Mann
Staffel-Stm.mm. / SS-Sturmm.
Staffel-Rottenf. / SS-Rottenf.
Staffel-U'Scharf. / SS-U'Scharf.
Staffel-Scharf. / SS-Scharf.
Staffel-O'Scharf. / SS-O'Scharf.
Staffel-H'Scharf. / SS-H'Scharf.
SS-U'Sturmf.
SS-O'Sturmf.
SS-H'Sturmf.
SS-Stubaf.
SS-O'Stubaf.
SS-Standartenf.
SS-Oberführer
SS-Brigadeführer
SS-Gruppenführer
SS-O'Gruppenf.

2. Einheit, Name und Vorname:
SS Pz.Gren.Schule 13./L.Rgt.
K ü r b i s, Herbert

3. a) Geburtstag: 13.12.1926
b) Geburtsort: Leuben
c) religiöses Bekenntnis: ev.
d) Staatsangehörigkeit: D.R.
e)

4. erlernter Beruf: Verwaltungs Angest. Jetzt: Waffen-SS
selbständig / priv. Dienst / öffentl. Dienst / Partei-Dienst

5. a) led., verw., gesch., verh. seit: mit
RB.-Nr. geboren:
b) Kinder: 1. m./w. 2. m./w. 3. m./w. 4. m./w. 5. m./w. 6. m./w. 7. m./w. 8. m./w. 9. m./w. 10. m./w.

6. Wohnort, Straße, Haus-Nr.

7. Größe: 1,69 Schuh-Nr.: 41 Kopfw.: 56

8. Einkommen bis 300.—, über 300.—, über 500.—, über 1000.— RM.

9. Sprachen und besondere Fähigkeiten:

10. Zivilstrafen:

11. Wehrnummer: Meißen 26/50/1/5
Nr. d. Erk.-Marke:

12. SS-Nummer:

13. SS-Auszeichnungen:
SS-Zivilabzeichen-Nr.:
Ehrendolch ja — nein
Ehrendegen ja — nein
Winkel ja — nein
Totenkopfring ja — nein

14. Sportabzeichen:
SA-Sportabz.
Reichssportabz.
Reitersportabz.
SS-Leistungsabz.
H.J.L.Silber

15. Parteiverhältnisse:
Partei-Eintritt:
Mitglieds-Nr.:
Gold. Parteiabz. ja — nein
Tod. Parteiabz. ja — nein
Blutorden ja — nein

16. Ausmärsche usw.:

Excerpts from a letter to Karl Genth from his girlfriend:

"*My dear, sweet Karli!*

...Today was a beautiful day. I mean as far as the weather is concerned. It would be much more beautiful if you were here. Whenever you are not with me, it is quite an entirely different feeling. Maybe you are still there in Kienschlag. I would be very happy if I knew, rather than imagining you are maybe somewhere out there in battle...

My darling, whenever we have a sweet, little baby and there is peace, and you can always be with me, it shall be wonderful. I do not want to make such beautiful plans for the future all the time, because as they say, rarely does anything come of it. Then again, whenever I think of this dreadful war that has destroyed all happiness, I cannot find any peace at all. The only consolation I have is that everyone is in God's hands, and everything happens as He wishes. And then I always think, why should our happiness and our future be destroyed, when we love each other so much and are eternally devoted...

I wish you the best, and good health, above all. Warm regards and thousands of passionate kisses from your beloved."

Karl Genth fell just three weeks later in Vogelsang!

The half of Karl Genth's identity tag.

Dienststelle
F.P.Nr. 26 667 L

O.U., 16.3.45

Betr.: Heldentod des SS-O.Gren. Karl G e n t h
geb. am 7. 3. 26 gefallen am 15.3.1945

An die

Dienststelle der

NSDAP in

[redacted]/ Magdeburg

Die Kp. bittet um Weiterleitung an den zustandigen Ortsgruppenleiter und baldigste Benachrichtigung der Eltern des Gefallenen.
Anschrift: Familie Karl G e n t h [redacted]/ Magdeburg

Heil Hitler !

SS-Untersturmführer
u. Kompanieführer

Dienststelle
F.P.Nr. 26 667 L

O.U., 16. 3. 45

Familie

Karl G e n t h

[redacted] / M a g d e b u r g

Sehr geehrte Familie Genth !

In dem Gefecht um VOGELSANG / Reg.Bez. FRANKFURT/Oder / am 15. 3. 1945 fiel Ihr Sohn Karl im Kampf um die Freiheit Grossdeutschlands in soldatischer Pflichterfüllung getreu seinem Fahneneid für Führer, Volk und Vaterland.
Zugleich im Namen seiner Kameraden spreche ich Ihnen meine wärmste Anteilnahme aus. Die Kompanie wird Ihrem Sohn stets ein ehrendes Andenken bewahren und in ihm ein Vorbild sehen.
Die Gewissheit, dass Ihr Sohn für die Grösse und die Zukunft unseres ewigen Deutschen Volkes sein Leben hingab möge Ihnen in dem schweren Leid, das Sie betroffen hat, Kraft geben und Ihnen ein Trost sein.

In aufrichtigem Mitgefühl
grüsse ich Sie mit

H e i l H i t l e r

[signature]

SS-Untersturmführer
u. Kompaniefuhrer

6./SS-Frw.Gren.Rgt. 86 — Lfd Nr. 144
(Komp., Batl., Regt., Div.)

Namentliche Verlustmeldung

an

ℌ-F. H. A. / Amt V, IIb

(dreifach)

1	Familienname		G e n t h
2	Vorname		Karl
3	Geburtstag, -ort, -kreis		7. 3. 26 [geschwärzt]
4	Dienstgrad		SS-Gren.
5	Erkennungsmarke		4./SS-Pz.Gren.A.u.E.Btl.
6	Familienstand		led. 12 -26084-
7	Ort, Tag und Zeitpunkt des Verl.		15.3.1945 Vogelsang
8	Gefallen[1])		Gra. Spl. Kopf
9	Verwundet[1])	schwer	—
		leicht	—
9a	Körperstelle u. Waffe[2])		—
10	Gefangen		—
11	Vermißt oder sonst.		—
12	Gestorben außerhalb der Lazarettbehandlung an	Verwundung	—
12a		Krankheit	—
12b		Unfall	—
12c		Selbstmord	—
12d		Vollstrecktes Todesurteil	—
13	Verbleib des Toten, Verwundeten oder Verletzten. An welche Sanitätsdienststelle abgegeben		beigesetzt Heldenfriedh. Fünfeichen / Oder Feld 2 Reihe 2
14	Genaue Grablage		Nr. 25 v. links
15	Letzter Wohnsitz (falls Berufssoldat, Heimatstandort des Friedenstruppenteils)		[geschwärzt] / b. Magdeburg
16	Anschrift der nächsten Angehörigen unter Angabe des Verwandtschaftsverhältnisses		Vater: Karl Genth wie 15

Bestell-Nr. W ℌ 4398
Metten & Co. Berlin SW 61

17	Angehörige benachrichtigt	16. 3. 45
18	Staatsangehörigkeit[2]	D.R.
19	Volkszugehörigkeit	
20	Einberufen durch ꞨꞨ-Erg.-Stelle	SS-Erg.St. Mitte XI
21	Eintritt in die Waffen-ꞨꞨ	30. 4. 43
22		
23		
24		

(Unterschrift)

SS-Ustuf. Kp. Fhr.

Raum für Skizze und Kampfbericht bei Vermißten oder Gefangenen

Grablage: Heldenfriedhof Fünfeichen / Oder

Feld 2
Reihe 2
Nr. 25

---

1) **Abkürzungen:** K. = Kopf, H. = Hals, Br. = Brust, Ba. = Bauch, R. = Rücken, l. A. = linker Arm, (I.G. = Inf.-Gesch., H.Gr. = Handgranaten-Verl., Gs.V. = Kampfstoffvergiftung, A.G. = Art.Gesch.).

2) Hierzu rechnen auch Verstauchung und Verrenkung durch stumpfe Gewalt infolge feindlicher Einwirkung, durch Verschüttung usw.

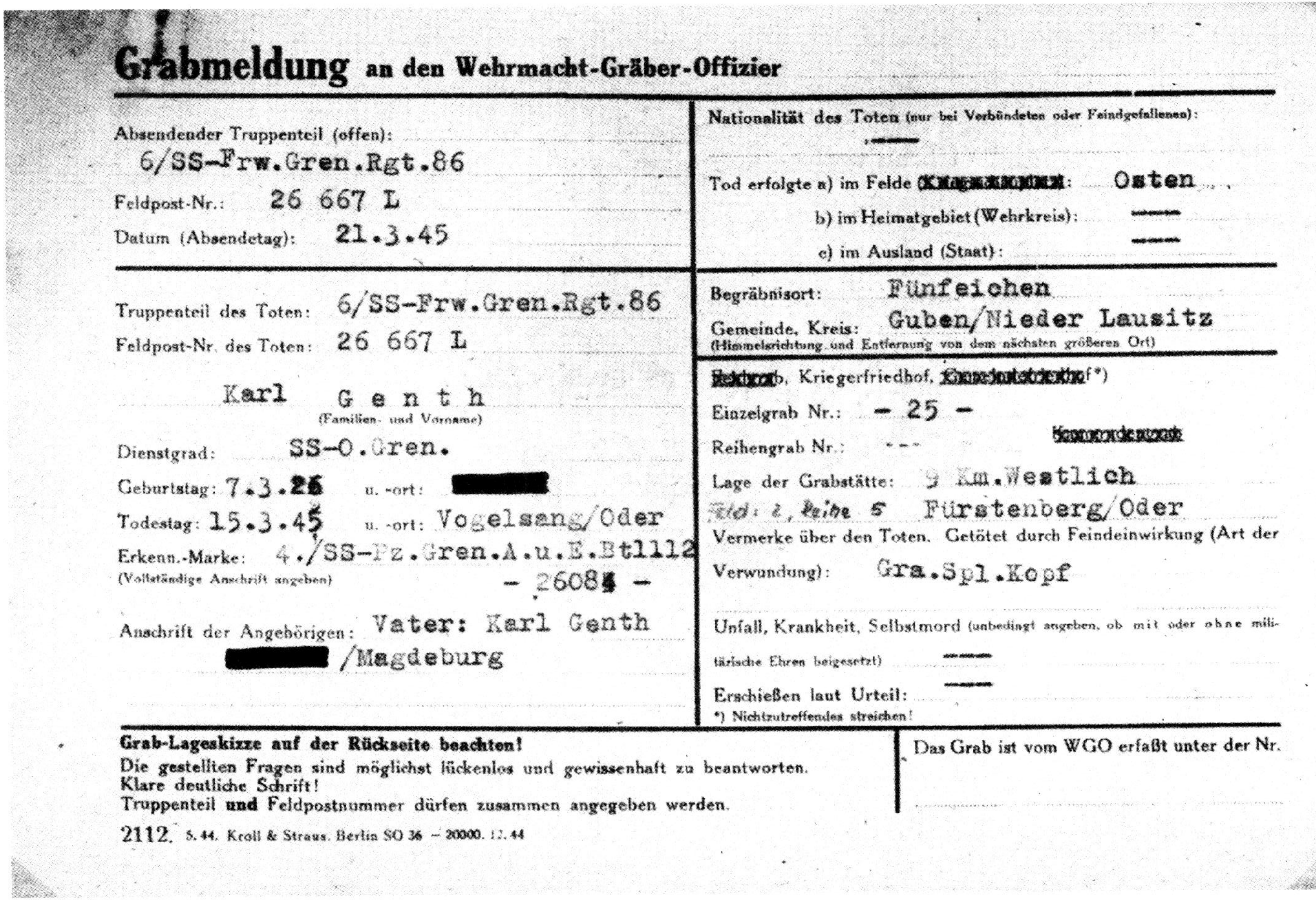

Grabmeldung an den Wehrmacht-Gräber-Offizier

Absendender Truppenteil (offen): 6/SS-Frw.Gren.Rgt.86

Feldpost-Nr.: 26 667 L

Datum (Absendetag): 21.3.45

Truppenteil des Toten: 6/SS-Frw.Gren.Rgt.86

Feldpost-Nr. des Toten: 26 667 L

Karl G e n t h
(Familien- und Vorname)

Dienstgrad: SS-O.Gren.

Geburtstag: 7.3.26 u. -ort: [illegible]

Todestag: 15.3.45 u. -ort: Vogelsang/Oder

Erkenn.-Marke: 4./SS-Pz.Gren.A.u.E.Btl112
(Vollständige Anschrift angeben) - 2608[illegible] -

Anschrift der Angehörigen: Vater: Karl Genth
[illegible] /Magdeburg

Nationalität des Toten (nur bei Verbündeten oder Feindgefallenen): —

Tod erfolgte a) im Felde ~~[illegible]~~: Osten

b) im Heimatgebiet (Wehrkreis): —

c) im Ausland (Staat): —

Begräbnisort: Fünfeichen

Gemeinde, Kreis: Guben/Nieder Lausitz
(Himmelsrichtung und Entfernung von dem nächsten größeren Ort)

~~[illegible]~~, Kriegerfriedhof, ~~[illegible]~~*)

Einzelgrab Nr.: - 25 -

Reihengrab Nr.: - - -

Lage der Grabstätte: 9 Km.Westlich
Feld: 2, Reihe 5 Fürstenberg/Oder

Vermerke über den Toten. Getötet durch Feindeinwirkung (Art der Verwundung): Gra.Spl.Kopf

Unfall, Krankheit, Selbstmord (unbedingt angeben, ob mit oder ohne militärische Ehren beigesetzt) —

Erschießen laut Urteil: —

*) Nichtzutreffendes streichen!

Grab-Lageskizze auf der Rückseite beachten!
Die gestellten Fragen sind möglichst lückenlos und gewissenhaft zu beantworten.
Klare deutliche Schrift!
Truppenteil **und** Feldpostnummer dürfen zusammen angegeben werden.

2112. 5.44. Kroll & Straus. Berlin SO 36 – 20000. 12.44

Das Grab ist vom WGO erfaßt unter der Nr.

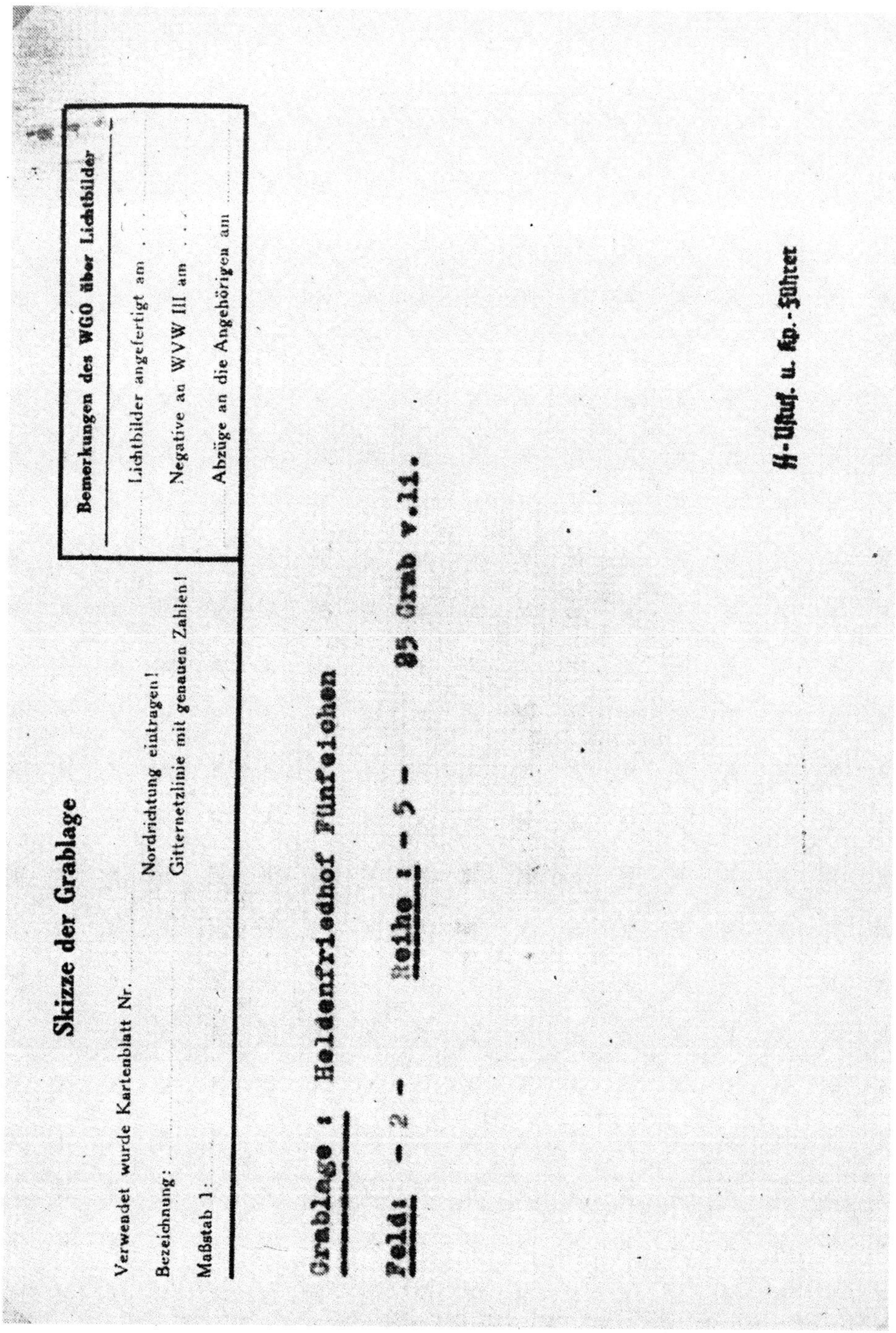

Skizze der Grablage

Verwendet wurde Kartenblatt Nr. ......

Bezeichnung: ...... Nordrichtung eintragen!

Maßstab 1: ...... Gitternetzlinie mit genauen Zahlen!

Bemerkungen des WGO über Lichtbilder

Lichtbilder angefertigt am ......

Negative an WVW III am ......

Abzüge an die Angehörigen am ......

Grablage : Heldenfriedhof Fünfeichen

Feld: - 2 - Reihe : - 5 - 85 Grab v.11.

SS-Ustuf. u. Kp.-Führer

Dienststelle
F.P.Nr. 26 667 L

O.U., 20. 3. 45

Gefallenen-Nachlass des

SS-Gren. G e n t h, Karl

1 Schuhputzzeugbeutel
1 Kleiderbürste
7 Stück Seife
2 Zahnpasta
2 Kämme
1 Füllhalter
1 Hautcreme
1 Handbürste
1 Pinzette
1 Spiegel
Schreibpapier
1 Notizbuch
1 Fotoalbum
1 Rasierpinsel
1 Taschentuch
1 Zahnbürste
1 Schere
1 Turnhose
1 Handschuh
1 Breiftasche m. Bildern
1 T"schenspiegel
1 Geldbörse mit Inhalt
1 Armbanduhr

F.d.R.:

SS-Hauptscharführer
u. Stabsscharführer

SS-Untersturmführer
u. Kompanieführer

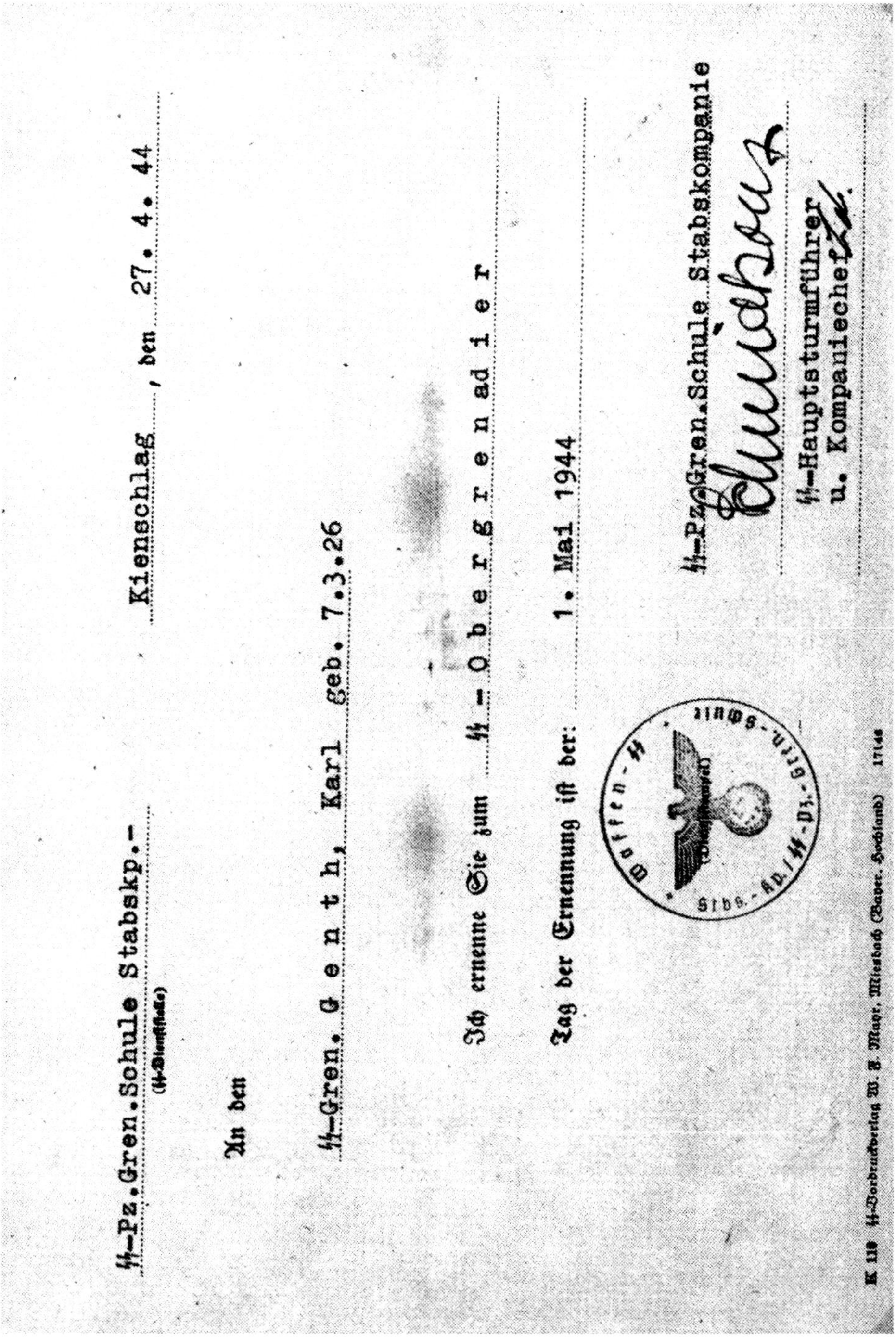

SS-Pz.Gren.Schule Stabskp.- Kienschlag, den 27. 4. 44
(SS-Dienststelle)

An den

SS-Gren. G e n t h, Karl geb. 7.3.26

Ich ernenne Sie zum SS - O b e r g r e n a d i e r

Tag der Ernennung ist der: 1. Mai 1944

SS-Pz.Gren.Schule Stabskompanie

SS-Hauptsturmführer
u. Kompaniechef.

Waffen-SS Stbs.-Abt./SS-Pz.-Gren.-Schule (Dienstsiegel)

K 118 SS-Vordruckverlag W. F. Mayr, Miesbach (Bayer. Hochland) 17146

SS-Panzer-Grenadier-Schule
Abt.Ib Az.:72 Hö./E.

Kienschlag, den 31.März 1944

Betr.: Abgabe einer Pistole.

An den SS-Schützen Genth Karl . . . . von der . Stabskompanie . .
wurde am heutigen Tage 1 Pistole. Sauer u.S. Kaliber 7,65 mm
Nr.. 373439 . mit Tasche verkauft und ausgehändigt,
(Preis RM 39.65)

Den Betrag erhalten:

SS-Sturm

Pistole empfangen:

SS-Schütze

6./SS-Frw.Gren.Rgt.86 O.U., 21. 3. 45

Betr.: Meldung von Vermissten, die zur Truppe zurückkehrten, bzw. deren Verbleib von der Kp. festgestellt werden konnte.
Bezug: Schriftl. Bef. Rgt. v. 21.3.45
An
II./SS-Frw.Gren.Rgt. 86

Lfd. Nr.:	Dienstgrad:	Name:	Vorname:	Geb. Datum:	Verbleib:
1	SS-Gren.	Wenzel	Philipp	15.6. 19	gefallen
2	"	Severinus	Andreas	18.10.08	Lazarett-Aufnahme
3	"	Brilsky	Rudolf	19.8. 27	Lazarett-Aufnahme
4	"	Jensen	Hans	26.4. 27	verbl.b. einer Wehrm.Ein
5	"	Rensing	Willi	3.10. 26	verbl. H.V.P. Treppeln
6	"	Szardin	Horst	9.10. 27	verbl. b.Wehrm.-Einheit

SS-Hauptscharführer
u. Stabsscharführer

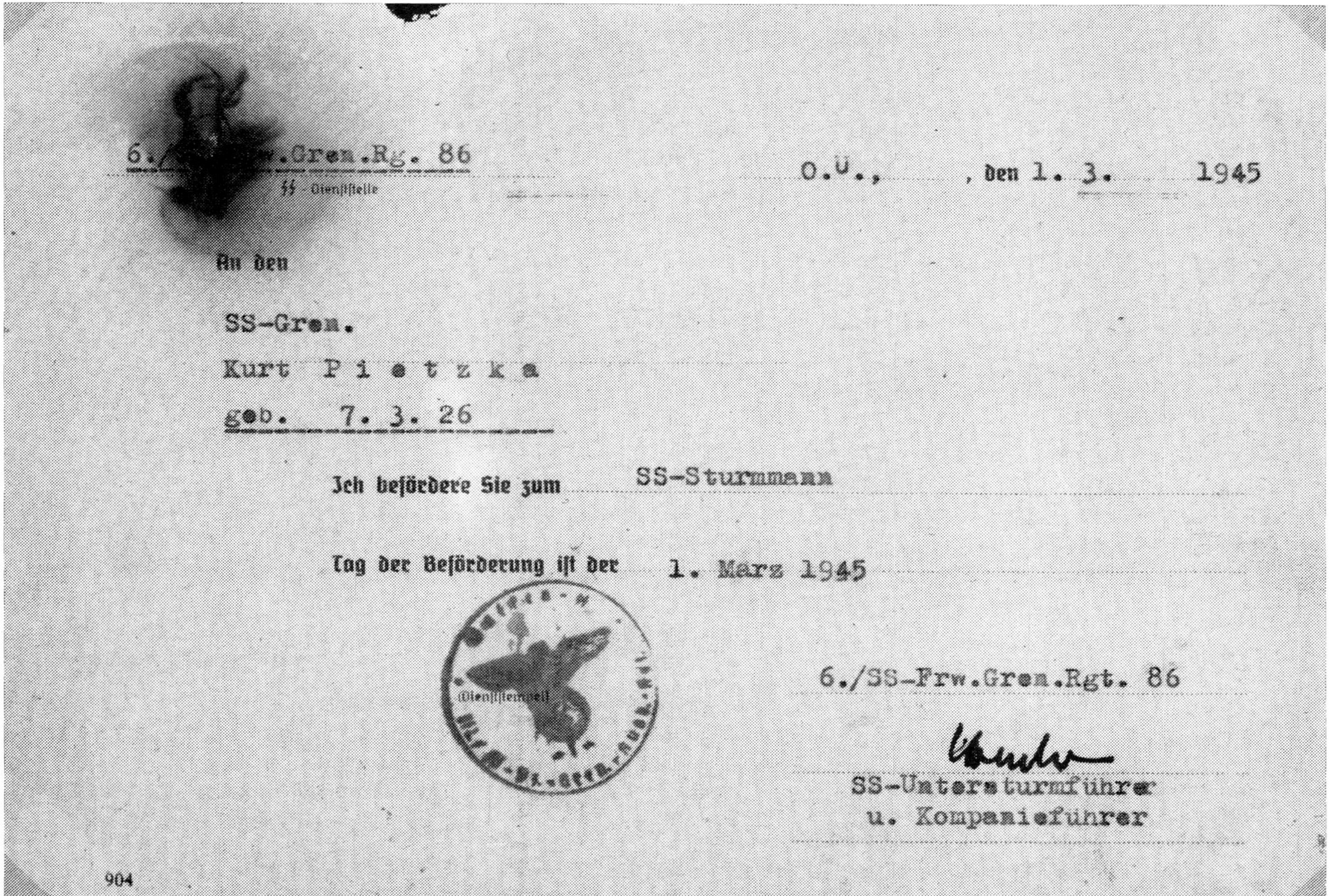

6./[illegible]w.Gren.Rg. 86
SS-Dienststelle

O.U., den 1. 3. 1945

An den

SS-Gren.
Kurt P i e t z k a
geb. 7. 3. 26

Ich befördere Sie zum SS-Sturmmann

Tag der Beförderung ist der 1. Marz 1945

Dienststempel

6./SS-Frw.Gren.Rgt. 86

SS-Untersturmführer
u. Kompanieführer

904

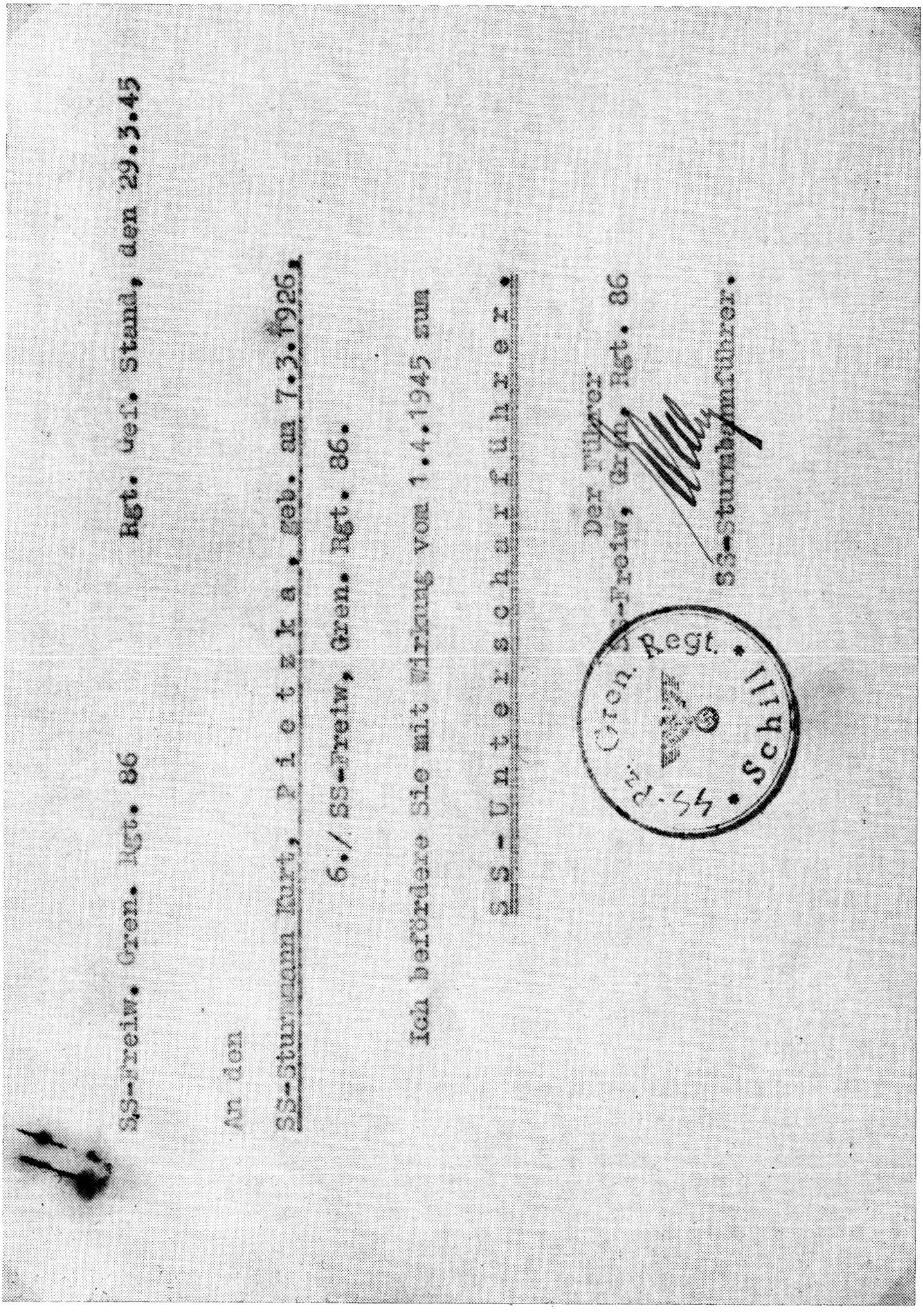

SS-Freiw. Gren. Rgt. 86 Rgt. Gef. Stand, den 29.3.45

An den

SS-Sturmmann Kurt, P i e t z k a , geb. am 7.3.1926.

6./SS-Freiw. Gren. Rgt. 86.

Ich befördere Sie mit Wirkung vom 1.4.1945 zum

S S - U n t e r s c h a r f ü h r e r .

Der Führer

SS-Freiw. Gren. Rgt. 86

SS-Sturmbannführer.

SS-Pz. Gren. Regt. • Schill •

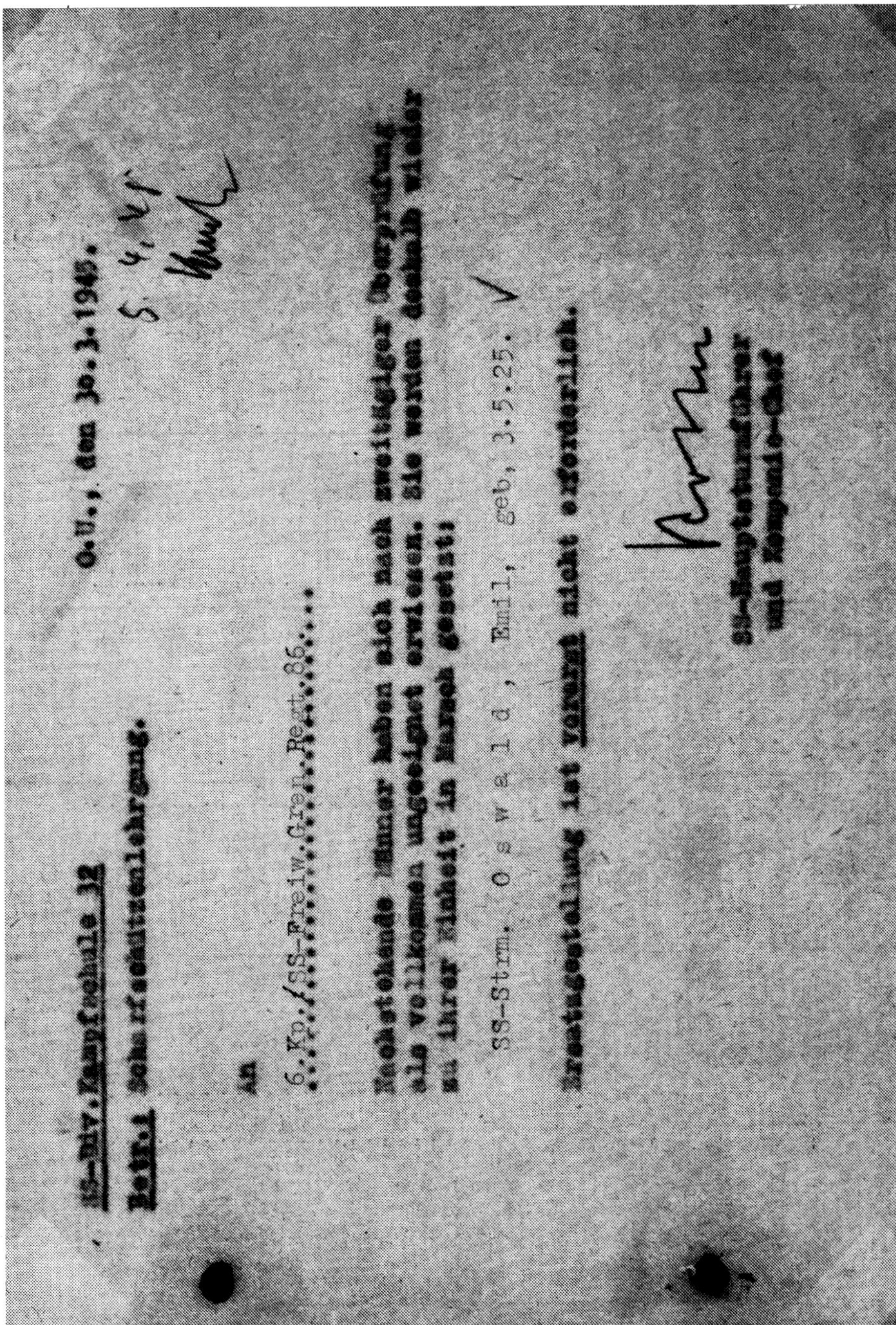

SS-Div.Kampfschule 32 O.U., den 30.3.1945.

Betr.: Scharfschützenlehrgang.

An

6.Kp./SS-Freiw.Gren.Regt.86....

Nachstehende Männer haben sich nach zweitägiger Überprüfung als vollkommen ungeeignet erwiesen. Sie werden deshalb wieder zu ihrer Einheit in Marsch gesetzt:

SS-Strm. O s w a l d , Emil, geb, 3.5.25.

Ersatzgestellung ist vorerst nicht erforderlich.

SS-Hauptsturmführer
und Kompanie-Chef

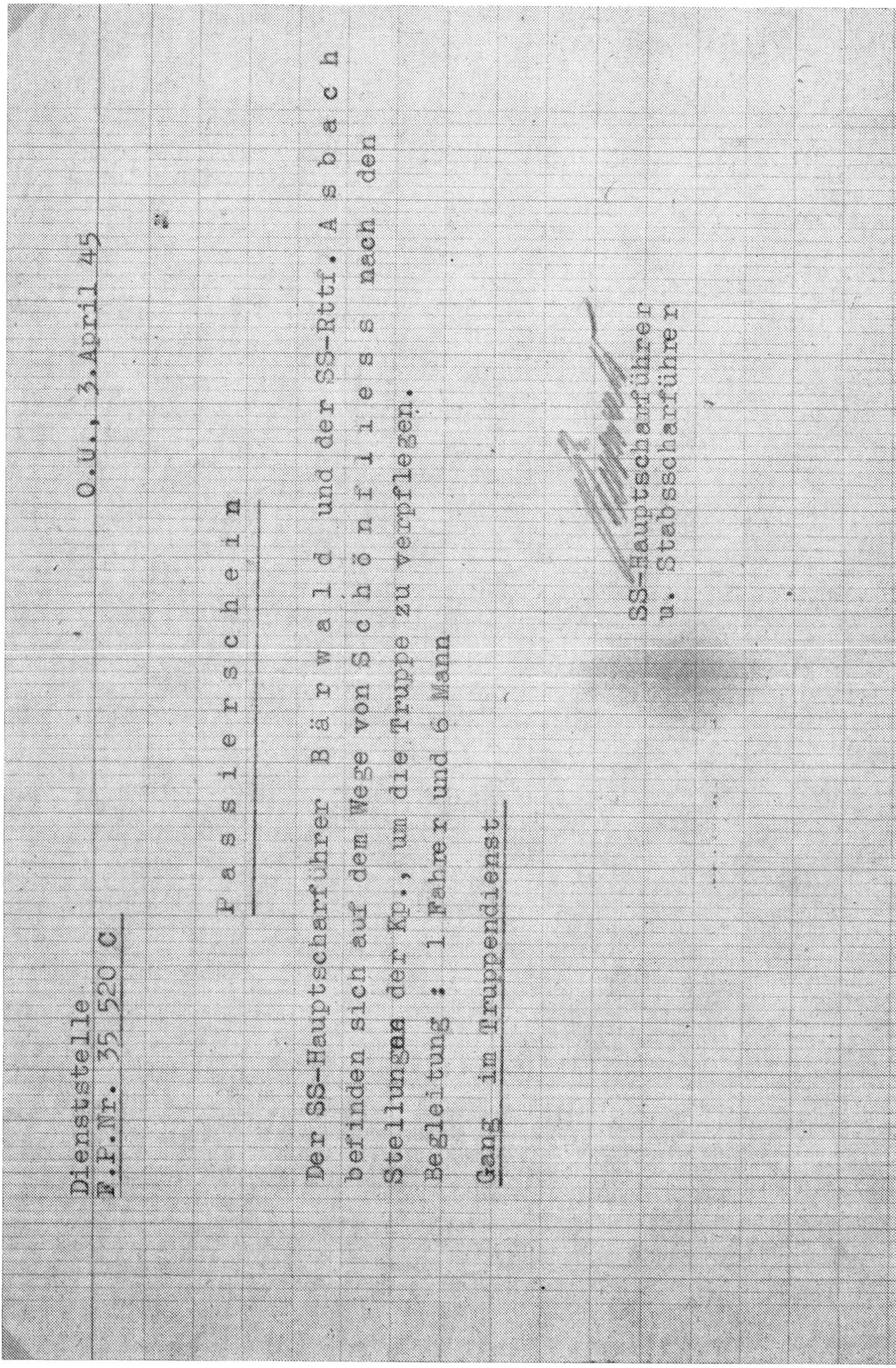

Dienststelle
F.P.Nr. 35 520 C

O.U., 3.April 45

Passierschein

Der SS-Hauptscharführer B ä r w a l d und der SS-Rttf. A s b a c h befinden sich auf dem Wege von S c h ö n f l i e s s nach den Stellungen der Kp., um die Truppe zu verpflegen.

Begleitung : 1 Fahrer und 6 Mann

Gang im Truppendienst

SS-Hauptscharführer
u. Stabsscharführer

SS-Freiw.Gren.Rgt.86 O.U., den 3.4.45.
Rgt.-Arzt

Betr.: Versetzung.

An Strm. F r u t s c h e r, Hans geb.am.28.4.13.

Sie werden ab sofort als Krankenträger zur 6.Komp. versetzt und versehen dort den Dienst des Kp.-SDG. an Stelle des ausgefallenen Uscha. Pietzka. Ihre Versetzung von der 13. zur 6. Komp. ist veranlasst.

Der Rgt.-Arzt:

SS.Hauptsturmführer

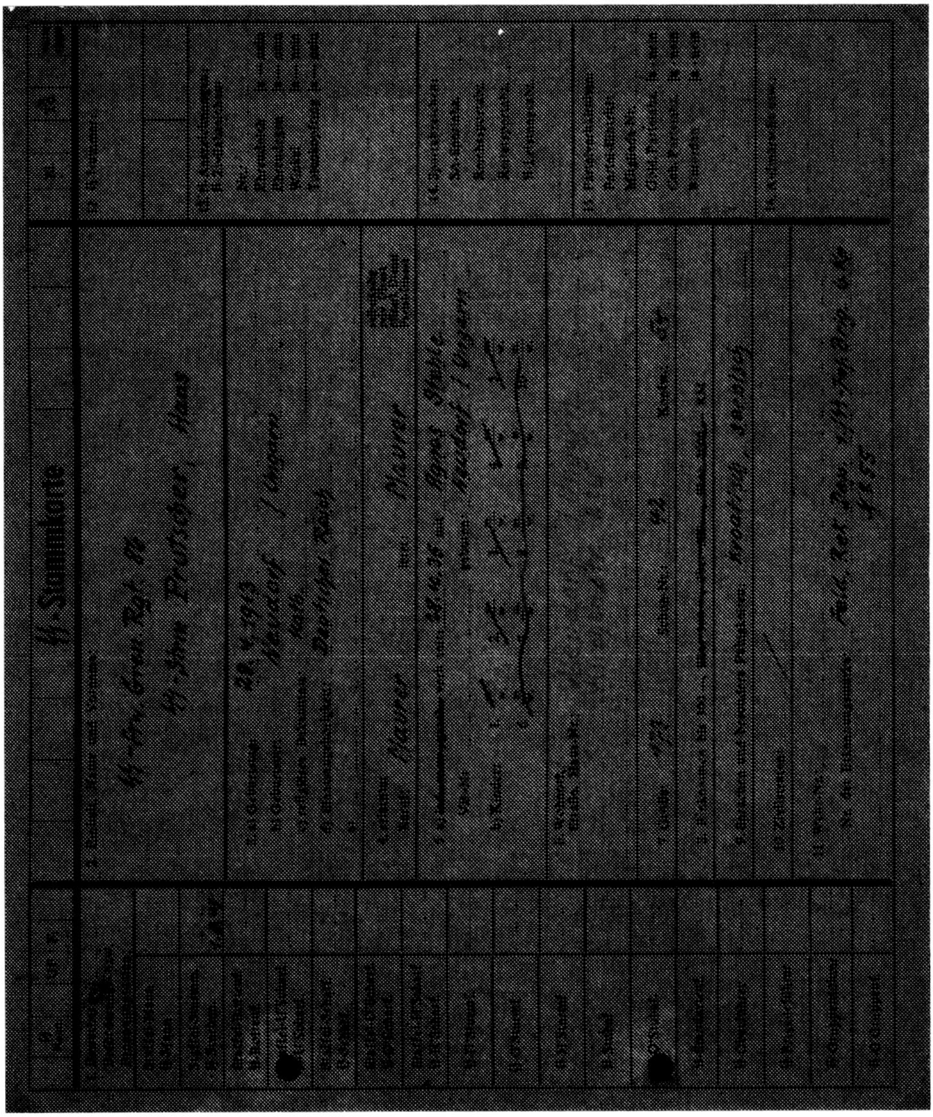

SS-Stammkarte

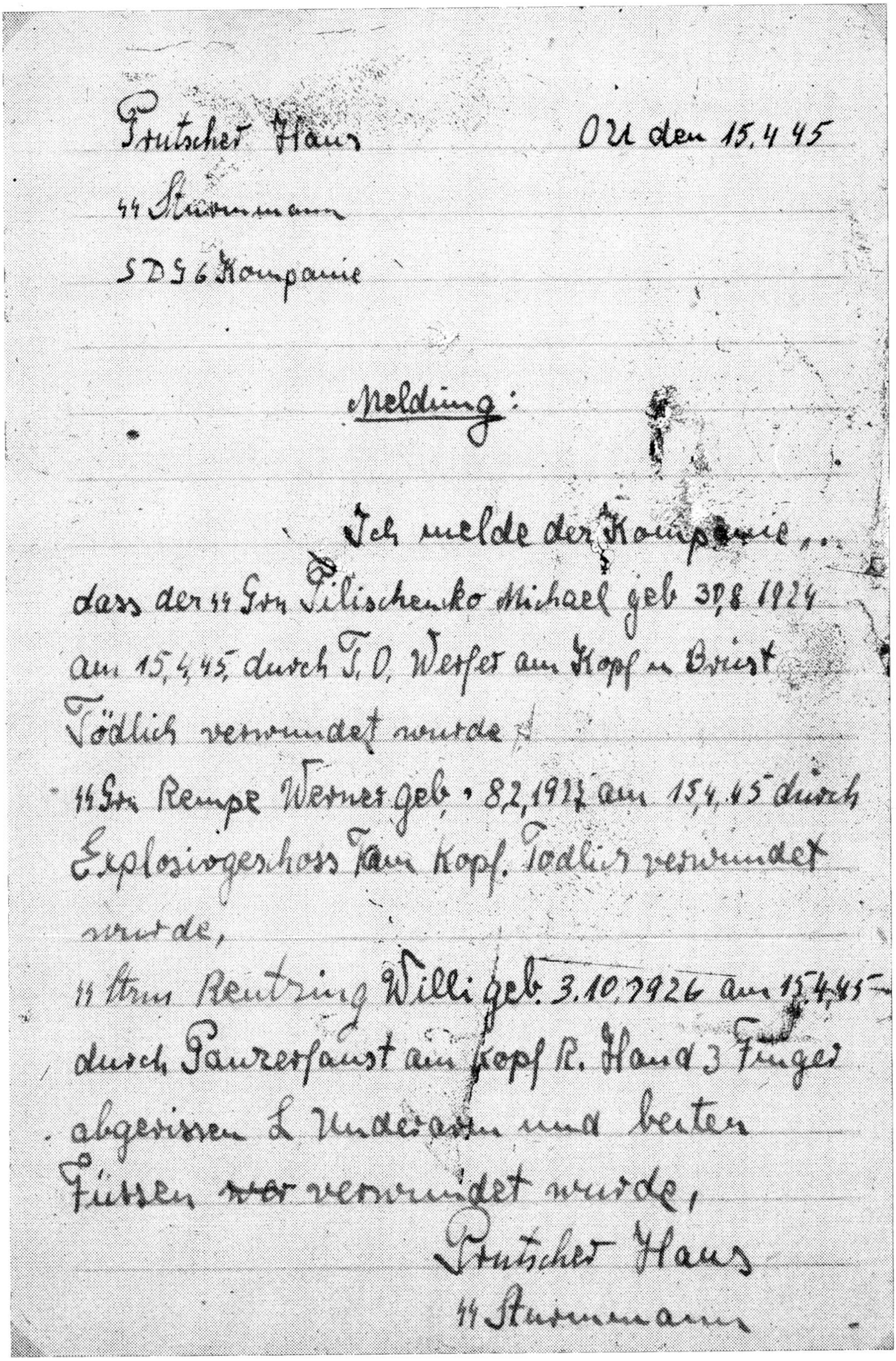

Deutscher Hans O.U. den 15.4.45

SS Sturmmann

SDG 6 Kompanie

<u>Meldung:</u>

Ich melde der Kompanie, ..

dass der SS Gren Pilischenko Michael geb 30.8.1924
am 15.4.45 durch T.O. Werfer am Kopf u Brust
Tödlich verwundet wurde.
SS Gren Rempe Werner geb. 8.2.1927 am 15.4.45 durch
Explosivgeschoss am Kopf. Tödlich verwundet
wurde,
SS Strm Reutzing Willi geb. 3.10.1926 am 15.4.45
durch Panzerfaust am Kopf R. Hand 3 Finger
abgerissen L Unterarm und beiten
Füssen ~~war~~ verwundet wurde,

Deutscher Hans
SS Sturmmann

6./SS-Frw.Gren.Rgt186 O.U., 4. 4. 1945

Betr.: Namentliche Meldung der Vermissten der 6./SS-Frw.Gren.Rg.. 86 seit dem Einsatz der Kp. im Ostraum.
Bezug: Rgt.-Tagesbefehl Nr. 9/45 Ziff. 4
Term.: 4.4. 1945
An
II./SS-Frw.Gren.Rgt. 86

Lfd. Nr.:	Dienst-grad:	Name:	Vorname:	Geb. Dat.:	vermisst: seit wann	vermisst: wo:
1	SS-Gren.	Vollmeyer	Werner	14.12.07	11.2.45	Vogelsang
2	SS-Gren.	Schilling	Heinrich	9. 3. 26	3. 3.45	"
3	SS-Gren.	Kenner	Paul	28.12.27	3. 3.45	"
4	SS-Gren.	Härtl	Richard	10.7. 26	11.2.45	"
5	SS-Gren.	Goyer	Franz	30.7. 09	11.2.45	"
6	SS-Gren.	Brügger	Christian	23.5.23	23.5.45	"
7	SS-Gren.	Schmiedeskamp	KarlHeinz	27.7126	4. 3.45	"
8	SS-Strm.	Hunger	Johann	26.4.22	11.2.45	"
9	SS-Rttf.	Matthias	Andreas	3.11.22	22.3.45	"
10	SS-Gren.	Salomon	Angeh. des 1. Ersatzes. Personalien konnten nicht festgestellt werden.			
11	SS-Gren.	Hinnen				
12	SS-Gren.	Wagner				

SS-Hauptscharführer
u. Stabsscharführer

den. 9.5.45.

An. Staabsscharf. 6 Kp.

Ich SS Strm. Packelmann. Gruppf. der Res. gruppe 6 Kp. Bitte sobald Post für die jenige Männer meiner Gruppe solte ankommen, mit dem Verpflegongswagen bei mir abgeben.

SS Strm. Packelmann.

Schönen gruß von Res. Grupp 6 Kp.

SS Strm. Packelmann Sepp.
" Windisch Franz.
" Bell georg.
" Horwarth Pongratius.
SS Gren. Bauerhenne Heinz.
" Kollmann Ernst.
" Dhiesse Heinrich.
" Schuh Josef.

SS Strm Packelmann.

6./SS-Frw.Gren.Rgt.86 O.U., 13.4.45

V o r s c h l a g zur V e r l e i h u n g des
K r i e g s v e r d i e n s t - K r e u z e s II. Klasse
mit Schwertern

SS-Uschа. Stiehler Erich geb.13.2.14 [redacted] Hauptgeräteverw.

Begründung: SS-Uscha. Stiehler ist seit dem 25.3.1945 Angehöriger der 6.Kp. und wurde innerhalb der Kp. als Hauptgeräteverwalter eingesetzt. St. hat während der Aufstellung des III./SS-Pz.Gren.Ausb.Rgt. seine Aufgaben als Hauptgeräteverwalter mit aussergewöhnlichem Fleiss, grosser Gewissenhaftigkeit und Eifer erfüllt. Während des Einsatzes der Kp. in der Slowakei sorgte St. unermüdlich für die Instandsetzung und Pflege der Waffen und Geräte, und versorgte die Kp. oft unter sehr erschwerten Bedingungen mit Munition, Waffen und Gerät. Jede ihm übertragene Arbeit führte er gut und gewissenhaft aus.
Auch während des derzeitigen Einsatzes der Kp. hat sich St. durch Instandsetzung, Pflege und Nachschub von Munition, Waffen und Gerät stets verdient gemacht.

Einsätze: Frankreich-Feldzug ganz
Osten von 22.6.41 – 9.9.41
Bandenbek.
Slowakei von 1.9. 44 –12.12.44
Osten seit 6.2.45

b.w.

Führungszeugnis

Der Gefreite Erich S t i e h l e r
(Dienstgrad, Vor- und Familienname)

geboren am 13. Februar 19 14

zu ████████
(Ort, Verwaltungsbezirk, Kreis)

hat vom 4. April 1934
(Tag des Diensteintritts)

bis zum 30. September 1936
(Tag der Entlassung)

gedient und sich während seiner Dienstzeit gut geführt.

Er wird in Ehren aus dem Heere entlassen.

Leipzig, den 30. 9. 1936
(Ort und Tag)

5. Kompanie
Inf.-Rgt. 11
(Truppenteil)

[signature]
(Unterschrift des Komp.- usw. Chefs)

Hauptmann u. Komp.-Chef
(Dienstgrad)

Form. Nr. 54. Friedrich Schumann Inh. Erich Schumann, Leipzig N 23

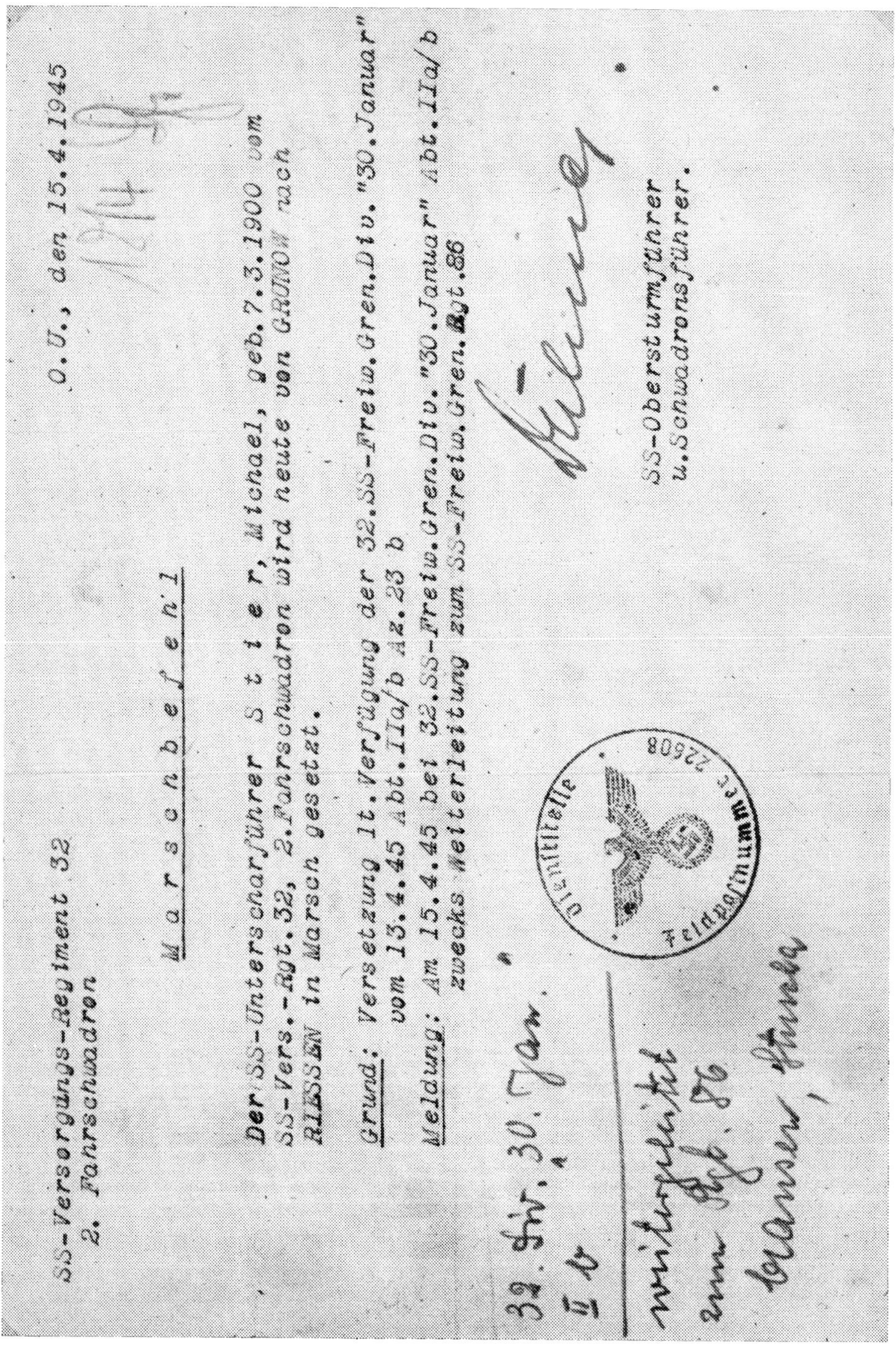

SS-Versorgungs-Regiment 32
2. Fahrschwadron

O.U., den 15.4.1945

M a r s c h b e f e h l

Der SS-Unterscharführer S t i e r, Michael, geb. 7.3.1900 vom SS-Vers.-Rgt.32, 2.Fahrschwadron wird heute von GRUNOW nach RIESSEN in Marsch gesetzt.

Grund: Versetzung lt. Verfügung der 32.SS-Freiw.Gren.Div. "30.Januar" vom 13.4.45 Abt.IIa/b Az.23 b

Meldung: Am 15.4.45 bei 32.SS-Freiw.Gren.Div. "30.Januar" Abt.IIa/b zwecks Weiterleitung zum SS-Freiw.Gren.Rgt.86

SS-Obersturmführer
u.Schwadronsführer.

Dienststelle
Feldpostnummer 22608

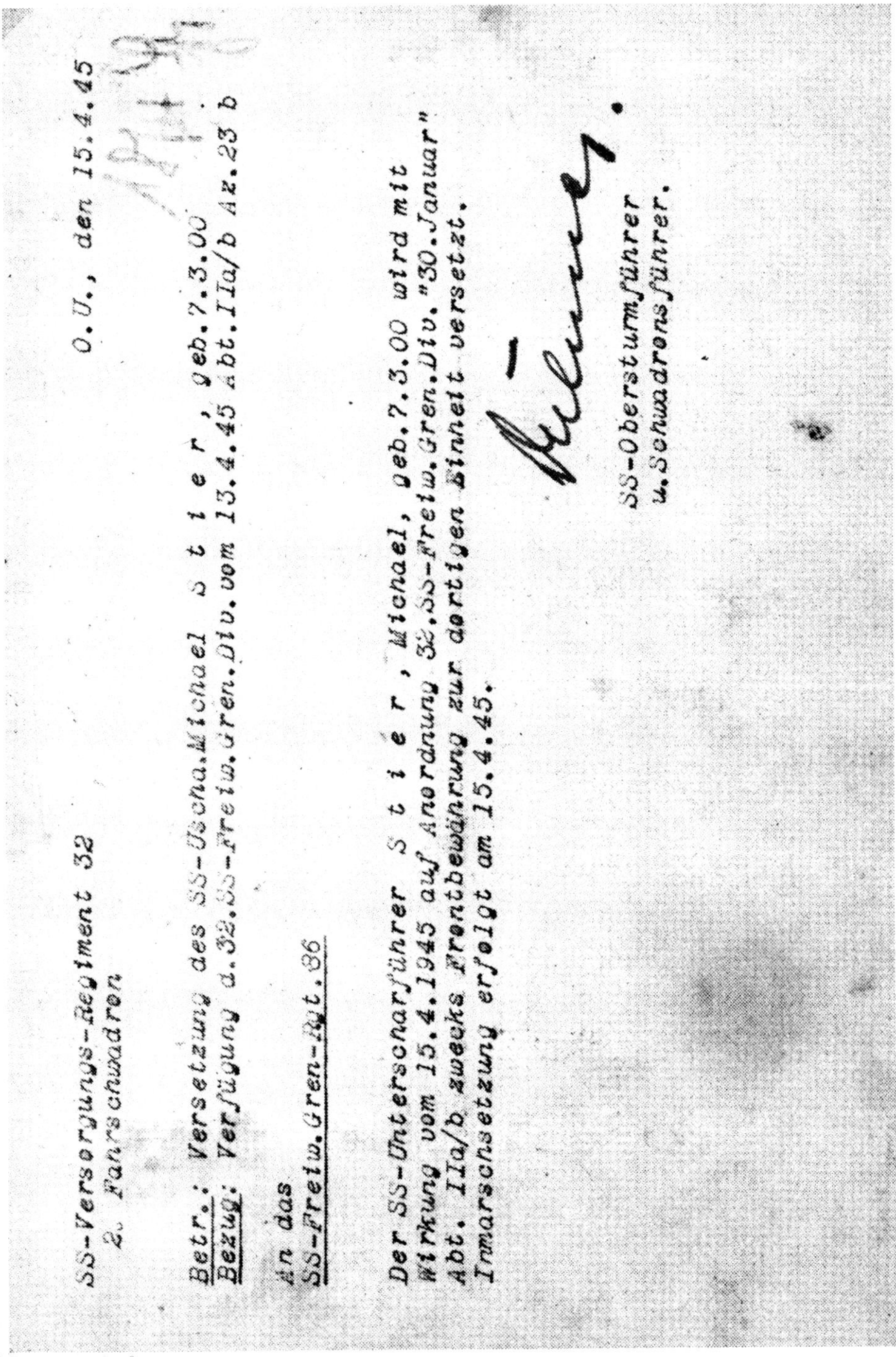

SS-Versorgungs-Regiment 32
2. Fahrschwadron

O.U., den 15.4.45

Betr.: Versetzung des SS-Uscha.Michael S t i e r , geb.7.3.00
Bezug: Verfügung d.32.SS-Freiw.Gren.Div.vom 13.4.45 Abt.IIa/b Az.23 b

An das
SS-Freiw.Gren-Rgt.86

Der SS-Unterscharführer S t i e r , Michael, geb.7.3.00 wird mit Wirkung vom 15.4.1945 auf Anordnung 32.SS-Freiw.Gren.Div."30.Januar" Abt. IIa/b zwecks Frontbewährung zur dortigen Einheit versetzt. Inmarschsetzung erfolgt am 15.4.45.

SS-Obersturmführer
u.Schwadronsführer.

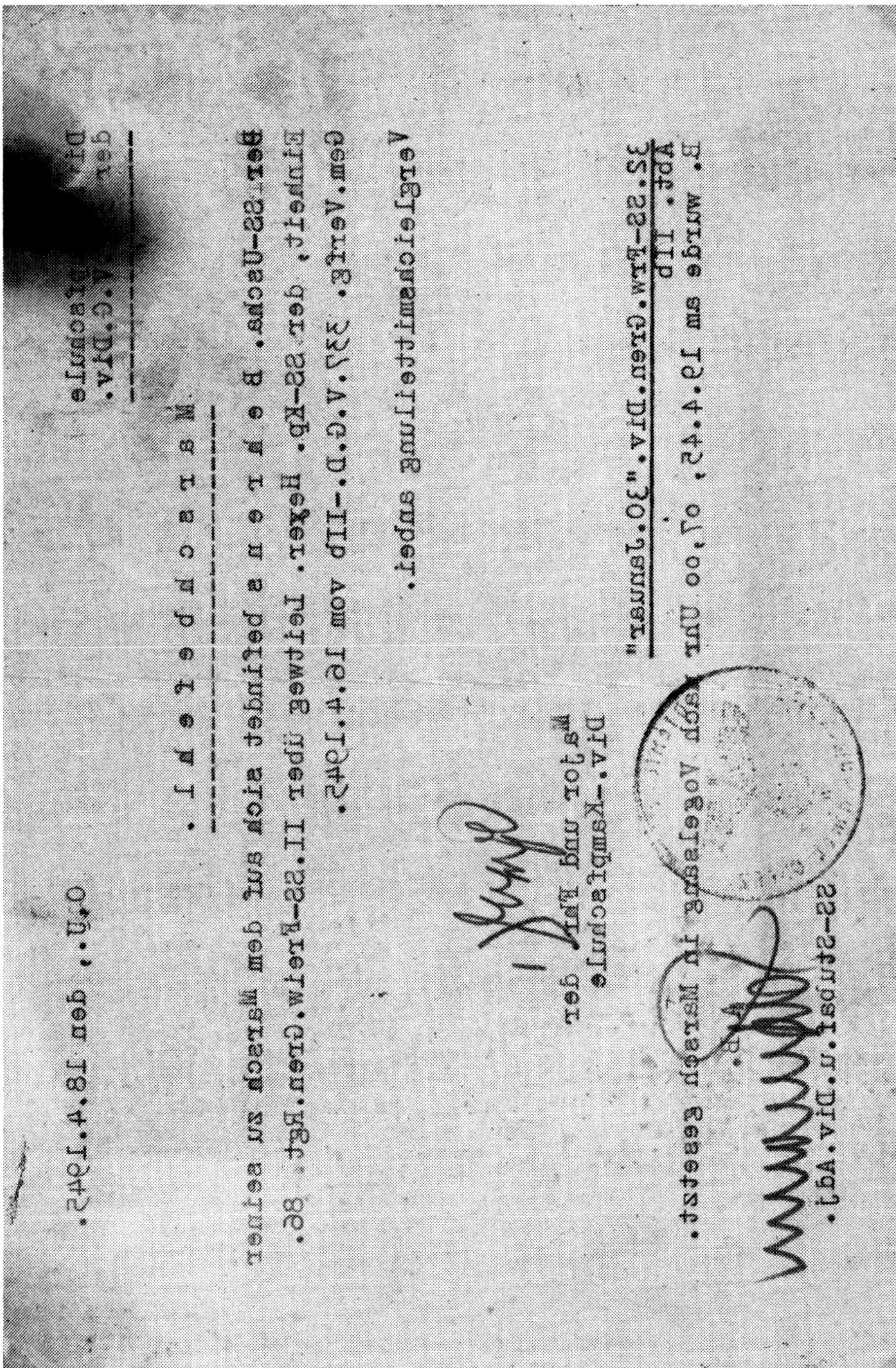

Div. … pfschule
der … V.G.Div.

O.U., den 18.4.1945.

Marschbefehl.

Der SS-Uscha. B e h r e n s befindet sich auf dem Marsch zu seiner Einheit, der SS-Kp. Hexer. Leitweg über II.SS-Freiw.Gren.Rgt. 86.
Gem.Verfg. 337.V.G.D.-IIb vom 16.4.1945.

Vergleichsmitteilung anbei.

Major und Fhr. der
Div.-Kampfschule

32.SS-Frw.Gren.Div."30.Januar"
Abt. IIb
B. wurde am 19.4.45, 07,00 Uhr nach Vogelsang in Marsch gesetzt.

A.B.

SS-Stubaf.u.Div.Adj.

lfd. Nr.	Dienstgr.	Name	Vor[name]	Geb. Dat.	Gefallen Datum	Urs[ache]	[Fr]iedhof	R.	N.	Benachr. am	Verlust m.	G.M.	Bemerk.
1.	44-Rttf.	Lagner	An[illegible]	12.7.22	6.2.45	[illegible]schuss	Fünfeichen	3	1	18.2.45	/	/	
2.	44-Uscha	Ickler	Wil[illegible]	11.11.22	8.2.45	Kopfschuss				18.2.45	/	/	Konnte nicht geborgen werden
3.	44-Gren.	Sauter	Werner	25.5.26	8.2.45	Bauchschuß	Fünfeichen	3	10	18.2.45	/	/	
4	44-Gren.	Hannemann	Werner	18.11.26	7.2.45	Halsschuß ~~unbekannt~~				18.2.45	/	/	Konnte nicht geborgen werden
5.	44-Strm.	Christmann	Alfons	25.9.26	8.2.45	Gra. Spl. Brust	Zillendorf		18	18.2.45	/	/	
6.	44-Strm.	Herale	Ambrosius	10.12.12	8.2.45	unbekannt				18.2.45	/	/	Konnte nicht geborgen werden
7.	44-Gren.	Dressler	Oswald	7.1.12	11.2.45	Gra. Spl. Kopf. Brust	Fünfeichen	3	9	18.2.45	/	/	
8.	44-Strm.	Graf	Leo	4.2.24	10.2.45	unbekannt	Fünfeichen	5	3	18.2.45	/	/	
9.	44-O.Gren.	John	Wolfgang	30.3.26	10.2.45	Kopfschuss ~~unbekannt~~				1.3.45	/	/	Konnte nicht geborgen werden
10.	44-Uscha	Wosnitza	Bruno	26.5.19	9.2.45 ~~26.5.19~~	unbekannt	Fünfeichen	6	10	26.2.45	/	/	
11.	44-Gren.	Lukas	Benno	18.5.26	21.2.45	Unfall Gra. Spl. Kopf	Fünfeichen	9	1	23.2.45	/	/	
12.	44-Gren.	Willich	Erwin	26.9.27.	10.2.45	unbekannt	Fünfeichen	9	6	26.2.45	/	/	
13.	44-Gren.	Frontzek	Friedel	[illegible]5.27.	1.3.45	Gra. Spl. Herz				10.3.45	/	/	nicht geborgen
14.	44-Strm	Moritz	Kurt	28.2.26	1.3.45	Gra. Spl. Kopf	Fünfeichen	8/5	24	10.3.45	/	/	
15.	44-Gren	Karpinski	Reinhold	26.3.27	4.3.45	Gra. Spl. Kopf	Fünfeichen	7/2	31	10.3.45	/	/	
16.	44-Sturm.	Kitzke	Friedrich	16.4.23	4.3.45	Gra. Spl. Hals	Fünfeichen	2/8	10	10.3.45	/	/	nicht geborgen
17.	44-Sturm.	Brinsky	Andreas	1.12.19	3.3.45	Gra. Spl. Hals	Fünfeichen	2/[illegible]	9	10.3.45	/	/	
18.	44-Gren.	Link	Anton	19.4.19	3.3.45	[illegible] Brust	Fünfeichen	2/2	7	10.3.45	/	/	
19.	44-Sturm.	Molenhauer	August	18.7.26	3.3.45	Gra. Spl. Brust	Fünfeichen	2/6	7	10.3.45	/	/	nicht geborgen

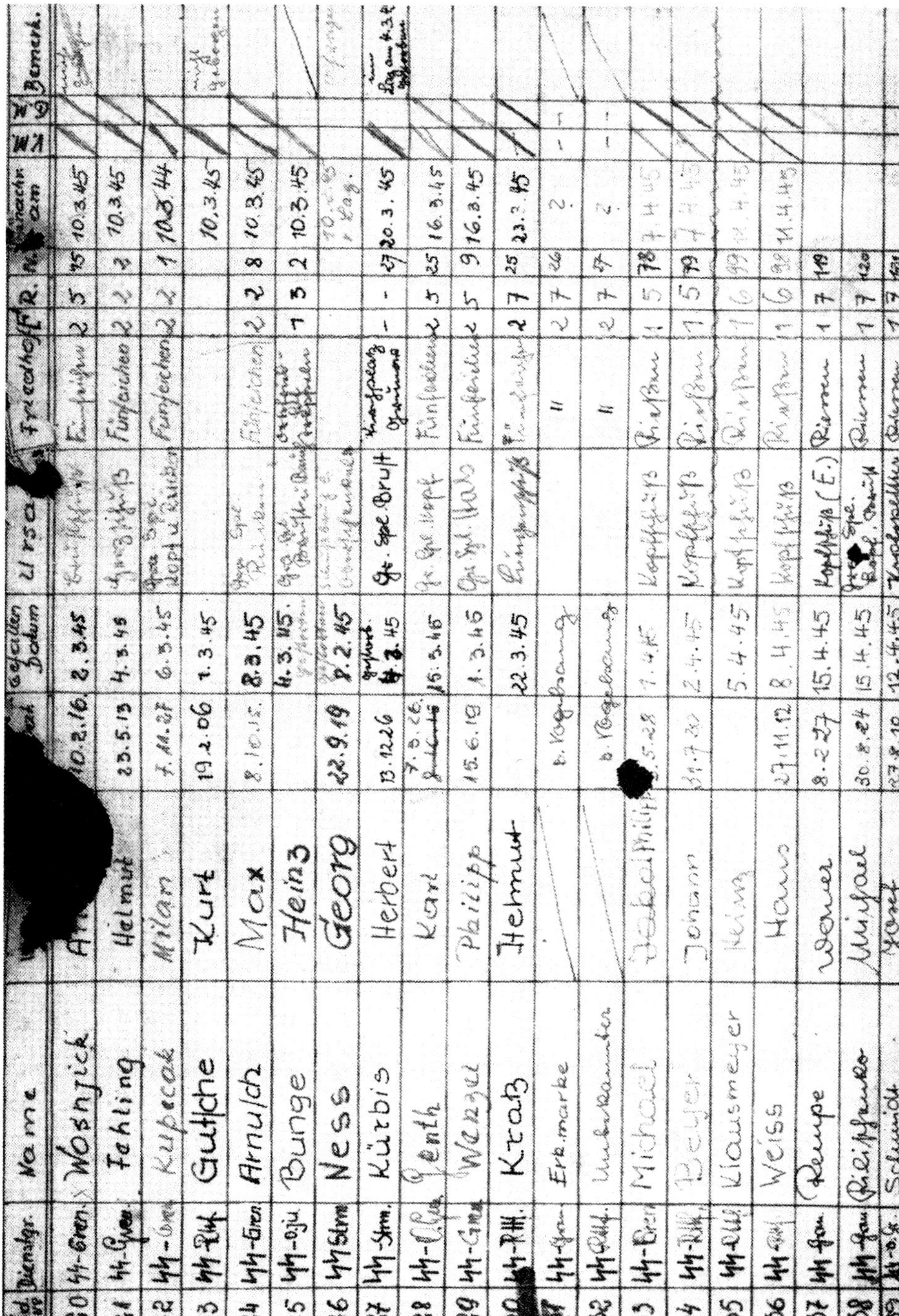

Lfd. Nr.	Dienstgr.	Name	Vorname	Geb. Dat.	gefallen Datum	Ursache	Friedhof	F	R.	Nr.	benachr. am	W.K.	W.D.	Bemerk.
20	SS-Gren.	Wosnjick	A[illegible]	10.2.16	2.3.45	[illegible]	Fünfeichen	2	5	75	10.3.45	/	/	[illegible]
21	SS-Gren.	Fehling	Helmut	23.5.13	4.3.45	[illegible]	Fünfeichen	2	2	3	10.3.45	/	/	
22	SS-Gren.	Kupecak	Milan	7.11.27	6.3.45	Gran. Spl. Kopf u. Rücken	Fünfeichen	2	2	1	10.3.44	/	/	
23	SS-Rttf.	Gutsche	Kurt	19.2.06	1.3.45						10.3.45	/	/	nicht geborgen
24	SS-Gren.	Arnulch	Max	8.10.15	8.3.45	Gran. Spl. Rücken	Fünfeichen	2	2	8	10.3.45	/	/	
25	SS-O.Ju.	Bunge	Heinz		4.3.45 [illegible]	Gr. Spl. [illegible]	[illegible]	1	3	2	10.3.45			
26	SS-Stm.	Ness	Georg	22.9.19	8.2.45	[illegible]					10.2.45 [illegible]			[illegible]
27	SS-Stm.	Kürbis	Herbert	13.12.26	gestorb. 4.3.45	Gr. Spl. Brust	[illegible]	–	–	27	20.3.45	/		[illegible]
28	SS-O.Gren.	Jenth	Karl	7.3.26	15.3.45	Gr. Spl. Kopf	Fünfeichen	2	5	25	16.3.45	/	/	
29	SS-Gren.	Wenzel	Philipp	15.6.19	1.3.45	Gr. Spl. Hals	Fünfeichen	2	5	9	16.3.45	/	/	
30	SS-Rttf.	Kraß	Helmut		22.3.45	[illegible]	Fünfeichen	2	7	25	23.3.45	/	/	
31	SS-Gren.	Erk.marke		b. Vogelsang			"	2	7	26	2	–	–	
32	SS-Rttf.	Unbekannter		b. Vogelsang			"	2	7	27	2	–	–	
33	SS-Gren.	Michael	[illegible] Philipp	[illegible].5.28	1.4.45	Kopfschuß	Riessen	1	5	78	7.4.45	/	/	
34	SS-Rttf.	Beyer	Johann	31.7.20	2.4.45	Kopfschuß	Riessen	1	5	79	7.4.45	/	/	
35	SS-O.Ltf.	Klausmeyer	Heinz		5.4.45	Kopfschuß	Riessen	1	6	99	11.4.45	/	/	
36	SS-Rttf.	Weiss	Hans	27.11.12	8.4.45	Kopfschuß	Riessen	1	6	98	11.4.45	/	/	
37	SS-Gren.	Rempe	Werner	8.2.27	15.4.45	Kopfschuß (E.)	Riessen	1	7	119				
38	SS-Gren.	Pilipenko	Michael	30.8.24	15.4.45	Gran. Spl. Kopf, Brust	Riessen	1	7	120				
39	SS-O.Sch.	Schmidt	Josef	27.8.10	12.4.45	Kopfsplitter	Riessen	1	7	121				

The Division's Emblem: the Tyr Rune.
The symbol of the Germanic God of War Ziu and the symbol for those who made a sacrifice in battle for their nation.

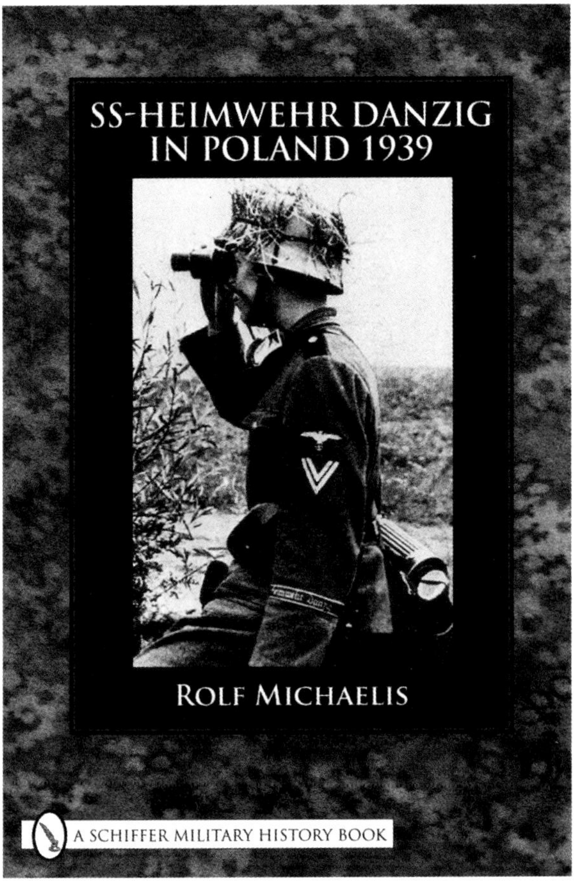

SS-Heimwehr Danzig in Poland 1939
Rolf Michaelis

This is the first book in English on this obscure early-World War II SS unit. In July 1939, SS-Heimwehr Danzig was formed from members of the III./4. SS-Totenkopf-Standarte "Ostmark," as well as from Danzig citizen volunteers. As a unit of the Reichsführer-SS they reinforced other existing Danzig units for the impending invasion of Poland. This book not only describes the political background that led to their deployment in September 1939, but also contains the combat recollections of former members, as well as over 100 photographs, and documents.

ISBN: 9780764329432

6"x9" over 140 bw images 112 pp hard cover

$29.95

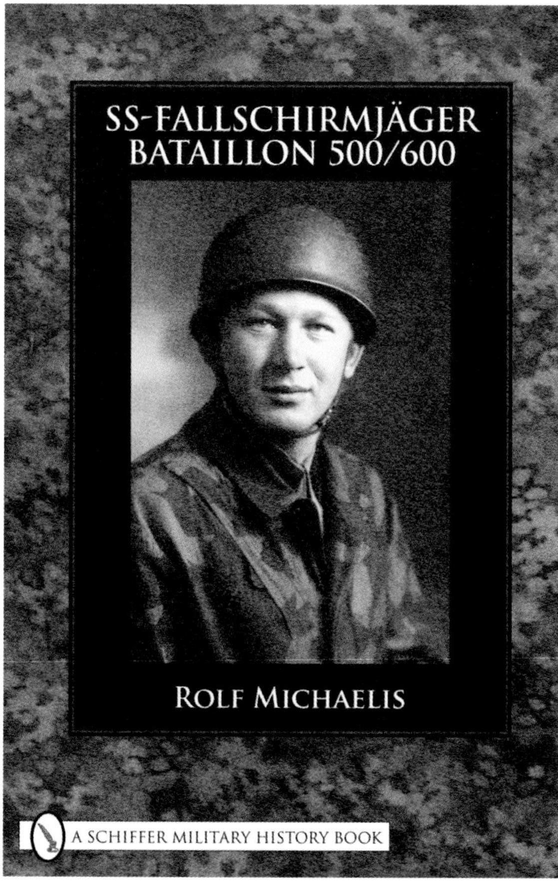

SS-Fallschirmjäger-Bataillon 500/600
Rolf Michaelis

This book is the history of the only Fallschirmjäger-Bataillon of the Waffen-SS during World War II. Formed in 1943 as a Bewährungsverband for special missions (guerrilla operations in the Balkans) the unit was deployed at many focal points of heavy combat on the eastern and western fronts. Nearly destroyed at the Schwedt and Alt-Küstrinchen bridgeheads, the remainder pulled back to the west over Parchim at the end of April 1945 and entered U.S. captivity in May 1945. This is their story, including extremely rare photographs.

ISBN: 9780764329449

6"x9" over 70 bw images 120 pp hard cover

$29.95